Choosing a
NAME FOR YOUR
BABY

Choosing a
NAME FOR YOUR
BABY

PENGUIN BOOKS

Penguin Books Australia Ltd
487 Maroondah Highway, PO Box 257
Ringwood, Victoria 3134, Australia
Penguin Books Ltd
Harmondsworth, Middlesex, England
Viking Penguin, A Division of Penguin Books USA Inc.
375 Hudson Street, New York, New York 10014, USA
Penguin Books Canada Limited
10 Alcorn Avenue, Toronto, Ontario, Canada M4V 3B2
Penguin Books (N.Z.) Ltd
182–190 Wairau Road, Auckland 10, New Zealand

First published by Penguin Books Australia Ltd 1992

10 9 8 7 6

Typeset in Cheltenham Book Condensed by Typeset Gallery Sdn. Bhd., Malaysia
Printed by Australian Print Group, Maryborough

National Library of Australia
Cataloguing-in-Publication data

Anderson, Felicity, 1963–

    Choosing a name for your baby.

    ISBN 0 14 016506 1.

    1. Names, Personal – Dictionaries. 1. Title. (Series:
Penguin pocket series).

929.4403

Contents

Introduction

~~~~~~

Names are important. They give a person an identity, an image and a sense of confidence. So make sure you take the time, in the months before the birth, to enjoy the pleasure of finding the right name for your very special baby.

Remember that the name you choose for your child should harmonise with your surname. Often a short given name goes well with a long surname and vice versa. A given name with an ending similar to the beginning of the surname – for example, Joshua Alexander – can sound awkward, as can names, such as Sally O'Malley, that are too alike.

Remember, too, that at school children are often given nicknames and abbreviations based on their names: you may love Alice but hate the shortened version Al. Richard Head may live to regret his parents' vagueness or naivety, and Donald Alan Grant and his sister Penelope Iris may find their initials the butt of many jokes!

A name that is the height of fashion today can quickly be outdated or inappropriate tomorrow. An unusual name can be charming to possess; an eccentric one will be a burden to bear. Remember, above all, that a name lasts a lifetime – and that a name wisely chosen is one of the most precious gifts you can give your child.

Introduction

GIRLS'
NAMES

A

Abbey *see* Abigail

Abella (Latin) beautiful

Abigail (Hebrew) a father's joy
Also Abaigael, Abbey, Abby, Abigal, Gail
See also Gail

Abra (Hebrew) mother of multitudes

Acacia (Greek) flower name

Ada (Old German) prosperous and happy
Also Adda, Aida, Eda, Etta

Adah (Hebrew) ornament

Adamina (Scottish) of the red earth
Feminine form of Adam

Adela (Old German) *see* Adèle

Adelaide (Old German) of noble rank
Also Adalia, Adaline, Adelaida, Adelheid, Adelia, Adelina, Adeline, Alina, Aline, Alyna
See also Adèle, Alice

Adèle (French) of noble cheer
Also Adela, Adelie, Adella, Adelle, Adila, Edila, Edla
See also Adelaide, Alice

Adeline *see* Adelaide

Adina (Aboriginal) good

Adnanuara (Aboriginal) running water

Adonia (Greek) beautiful, goddess-like lady
Feminine form of Adonis

Adriana (Latin) woman of the Adriatic
Feminine form of Adrian
Also Adria, Adriane, Adrianna, Adrianne, Adrienne

Adrienne (French) *see* Adriana

Affrica (Celtic) pleasant

Agatha (Greek) good, kind woman
Also Agace, Agacia, Agafia, Agata, Agathe, Agathy, Agueda

Aglaia (Greek) splendour, beauty;
one of the three Graces – goddess
of harmony
Also Aglae

Agnes (Greek) pure, chaste
Also Agna, Agnella, Agnese, Agneta,
Agnete, Agnies, Agnyta, Aigneis,
Aneda, Anese, Annais, Anneyce,
Annis, Annys, Ines, Inesita, Inez,
Nesta, Neysa, Neza, Ynes, Ynez

Agnies (French) *see* Agnes

Agnola (Italian) *see* Angela

Agostina (Italian) *see* Augusta

Ah Cy (Chinese) lovely

Ah Lam (Chinese) like the orchid

Aileen (Anglo–Irish) *see* Helen

Ailsa (Scottish) of good cheer
Also Aillsa, Ailssa, Elsa, Ilsa

Aimée *see* Amy

Ainsley (Old English) clearing or
meadow
Also Ainslea, Ainslee, Ainsleigh,
Ainsly, Anslea

Airlia (Greek) ethereal

Aithne [eth-ni] (Celtic) little fire
Also Eithne, Ethene, Ethne

Akala (Aboriginal) parrot

Akuna (Aboriginal) to know or follow

Alana (Celtic) beautiful, harmonious
one
Feminine form of Alan
Also Alaine, Alanah, Alanna,
Alanne, Alayna, Alayne, Aleine,
Alina, Aline, Allene, Allyn, Lana,
Lane, Lanna

Alatea (Spanish) truth

Alba (Aboriginal) wind

Alberta (Old German) noble and
bright
Feminine form of Albert
Also Albertina, Albertine,
Albertyna, Albrette, Elberta

Albinia (Latin) *see* Elvira
Also Alba, Albigna, Albina

Alda (Old German) old

Alethea (Greek) truth
Also Alatea, Aleethea, Aletea,
Aletha, Aletheia, Alithea

Aletta (Latin) winged or bird-like
Also Aleta, Alette, Alida, Alita, Alouetta

Alexandra (Greek) helper and protector of mankind
Feminine form of Alexander
Also Alejandra, Aleksandrina, Alessandra, Alexa, Alexandraine, Alexandria, Alexandrina, Alexandrine, Alexia, Alexina, Alexine, Alexis, Alix, Elexa, Sacha, Sandra, Sondra, Zandra

Alexia *see* Alexandra

Alexis *see* Alexandra

Alfreda (Old German) elf counsel
Feminine form of Alfred
Also Albreda, Alfreta

Alice (Old French) noble and kind
Also Ailis, Aleece, Alesia, Alicen, Alicia, Alis, Alisa, Alise, Alison, Alisone, Alisoun, Alisson, Alize, Allis, Allisa, Allissa, Allysa, Allyson, Alson, Alyce, Alys, Lycia
See also Adelaide, Adèle

Alicia *see* Alice

Alina (Latin) *see* Adelaide (Adeline)
See also Alana

Alison (Gaelic) *see* Alice

Alivia (Old English) alive

Alix (French) *see* Alexandra

Alkira (Aboriginal) sky

Alla (Old English) the only one

Allegra (Italian) joyful and cheerful

Allira (Aboriginal) quartz

Alma (Latin) fair or kind

Almira (Arabic) princess
Also Almeria, Elmira, Mira

Aloha (Hawaiian) greetings, farewell, love and kindness

Alouetta (Al-oh-etta) *see* Aletta

Alpha (Greek) the first

Althea (Greek) wholesome, a healer
Also Althaea, Althee, Altheta, Thea

Alvira *see* Elvira

Alwyn (Old German) elf friend

Alysia (Greek) possessive
Also Alisa, Alisia, Alysa

Alyssa (Greek) flower name, Alyssum

Alzena (Arabic) woman

Amabel *see* Mabel

Amanda (Latin) worthy of love

Amara (Greek) unfolding

Amara (Sanskrit) immortal

Amaranth (Greek) fading flower
Also Amarantha

Amarina (Aboriginal) rain

Amaryllis (Greek) country girl;
sparkling stream
Also Amarilla, Amarillis, Amaryl,
Marilla

Amata (Latin) *see* Amy

Amber (Egyptian) light

Amelia (Old German) *see* Emily

Amena (Old French) yielding

Amethyst (Greek) of the colour of
wine

Aminar (Arabic) honest, faithful

Aminta (Greek) protected

Amity (French) friendly

Amy (French) beloved
Also Aimée, Amata, Amaya, Ame,
Amia, Amice, Amie, Amieia, Amina,
Amity, Amoretta, Amorita, Amye,
Esmé, Esmée

Anais (English) *see* Anne

Anastasia (Greek) resurrection
Feminine form of Anastasius
Also Anastasie, Anastassia,
Anastatia, Anastazia, Anestasia,
Anstace, Anstey, Anstice, Anstyce,
Nastassia, Nastssja, Nastassla,
Nastasya, Nastaya, Nastya,
Nastyenka, Stacia, Stacie, Stacy,
Tasia

Andrea (Greek) womanly
Feminine form of Andrew (Andreas)
Also Aindrea, Andreana, Andrée,
Andria, Andriana, Andrina

Angela (Greek) a heavenly
messenger
Feminine form of Angel
Also Agnola, Aingeal, Angel, Angele,

Angeletta, Angelina, Angeline, Angelita, Angiola, Aniela, Anjela, Engel, Engelchen

Angelica (Latin) angelic
Also Angelika, Angelique, Angyelika

Angelina (English) *see* Angela

Anh (Vietnamese) a flower

Anita *see* Anne

Annabel (Scottish) *see* Mabel (Amabel)

Anne (Hebrew) full of grace
Also Ana, Anais, Anca, Aneta, Anica, Anita, Ann, Anna, Annan, Annetta, Annette, Annie, Annika, Annina, Annuschka, Anona, Chana, Channa, Hana, Hanicka, Hanita, Hannah, Hannette, Nan, Nancy, Nanette, Nanny, Nina, Ninette, Nita, Ona, Vanka

Annette (French) *see* Anne

Annora *see* Honor

Anthea (Greek) lady of the flowers
Also Anthia, Bluma, Thea, Thia

Antigone (Greek) contrary, born against

Antoinette (French) *see* Antonia

Antonia (Italian) inestimable, beyond price
Feminine form of Anthony (Antony)
Also Anthonia, Antoinette, Antonette, Antoni, Antonya, Netta, Netti, Netty, Toinette, Toni, Tonya

Aphra (Hebrew) dust
Also Afra

Appolline (Greek) of Apollo
Also Apollonia

April (Latin) the open
Also Avril

Arcadia (Greek) peaceful and happy

Areta (Greek) holy, virtuous, divine
Also Arete, Aretha, Aretta, Arette

Ariadne (Greek) the very holy one
Also Ariadna, Ariane, Arianna

Ariel (Hebrew) lioness of God
Also Ariella, Arielle

Arilpa (Aboriginal) moon

Arizona (North American Indian) little creeks

Arleen (Old German) a pledge

Armida (Persian) beautiful sorceress

Armilda (Latin) braceleted

Arnurna (Aboriginal) blue water lily

Arora (Aboriginal) cockatoo

Arrabel (Scottish) *see* Mabel (Amabel)

Asha (African) life
Also Aisha

Ashleigh (Old English) of the ash tree
Also Ashlee

Aspasia (Greek) welcome

Asta (Greek) a star

Astrid (Old German) divine strength

Asura (Sanskrit) spiritual

Atalanta (Greek) swift runner
Also Atalante, Atalanti, Attalanta

Atalaya (Spanish) watcher, guardian
Also Ataliah, Atalya, Talia, Talya

Athanasia (Greek) undying, immortal

Athena (Greek) wisdom
Also Athene

Audrey (Old English) noble strength
Also Audrea, Audree, Audrie, Audrye, Etheldreda

Augusta (Latin) the high, honoured, mighty
Feminine form of Augustus
Also Agostina, Augusteen, Augustina, Augustine, Austina, Austine, Gus, Gussie, Gusta, Tina

Aurelia (Latin) golden lady
Also Aralie, Aurea, Aurel, Aurelie

Aurora (Latin) dawn
Also Aurore, Ora

Ava (Greek) eagle

Aveline (Hebrew) pleasant

Averil (Old English) sacred wild boar

Avicia (German) *see* Avis

Avis (Old German) bird-like
Also Aricia, Avice, Avicia

Ayesha (Persian) happy

Azalea (Old German) of noble cheer
Also Azaleah

Azaria (Hebrew) blessed by God
  Feminine form of Azariah
  Also Azeria, Zaria

Aziza (African) gorgeous

Azura (Persian) sky blue

B

Babette (French) *see* Barbara

Bakana (Aboriginal) lookout

Baptista (Old French) one who baptises
Feminine form of Baptist
Also Baptysta, Batista, Battista

Bara (Aboriginal) dawn

Barbara (Greek) stranger
Also Babette, Babica, Barbe,
Barbrischa, Barbro, Baruska,
Varenka, Varina, Varvara

Barite (Aboriginal) girl

Basia *see* Basilia

Basilia (Greek) royal
Feminine form of Basil
Also Basia, Basilea, Basilie, Basilla

Bassania (Greek) realm of the sea

Bathsheba (Hebrew) daughter of a vow
Also Sheba

Beatrice (Latin) she who brings joy
Also Beatrix, Beatriz, Beatty, Blaza,
Blazena, Trixie

Bebe (French) baby

Beka (Hebrew) half-sister
Also Becca, Bekah, Bekka

Belinda (Old German) wise serpent
Also Belynda
See also Linda, Melinda

Belisama (Gaelic) queen of heaven

Belle (French) beautiful
Also Bell, Bella
See also Elizabeth (Isabel), Mabel
(Annabel, Arrabel), Mirabel

Belvina (Latin) fair one
Also Belva, Belvia

Benedicta (Latin) the blessed
Feminine form of Benedict
Also Benedetta, Benedikta, Benetta,
Benicia, Benita, Benoîte

Benita (Spanish) *see* Benedicta

Berengaria (Latin) a bear, spear
Feminine form of Berenger

Berenice (Greek) bringer of victory
Also Berneice, Bernice, Berniz,
Berrice

Bernadette (Old German) as brave
as a bear
Feminine form of Bernard
Also Bernadina, Bernadine,
Bernadot, Bernadotte, Bernetta,
Bernita, Burnette

Bertha (Old German) the bright
Also Berta, Berthe, Bertilia, Bertina,
Bertine

Beryl (Greek) precious jewel,
precious stone
Also Beryle, Berylla

Bessie *see* Elizabeth

Beth *see* Elizabeth

Bethany (Hebrew) worshipper of God
Also Bethanie

Bethia (Hebrew) daughter of
Jehovah

Bettina *see* Elizabeth

Beulah (Hebrew) to be married
Also Beula, Beulie

Beverley (Old English) from the
beaver's stream
Also Beverlie

Bianca (Italian) *see* Blanche

Bibiana (Latin) full of life
Also Bibi, Viviana

Bijou (French) jewel

Birget (German) *see* Bridget

Birgitta (Scandinavian) *see* Bridget

Blanche (French) white
Also Bianca, Bijanka, Blanca,
Blanch, Blanka, Bluinse, Branca

Blasia (Latin) the babbler

Bliss (Old English) felicity,
happiness

Blodwen (Welsh) white flower

Blythe (Old English) happy and
joyous

Bo (Chinese) precious

Bobbette *see* Roberta

Bonnie (Latin) good
  Also Bona, Bonita, Bonny

Branwen (Welsh) dark-haired
  beauty

Breanna *see* Bryony

Brenda (Old English) fire-brand or
  sword

Brenna (Celtic) dark-haired

Briana (Celtic) woman of strength
  Feminine form of Brian
  Also Brianna, Brienne

Bridget (Celtic) the highest strength
  Also Bedelia, Beret, Bride, Bridgid,

Bridie, Brie, Bries, Brietta, Briganti,
Brigette, Brighid, Brigid, Brigida,
Brigide, Brigit, Brigita, Brigitta,
Brigitte, Brigyta, Brischia, Brit,
Brita, Britt, Britta

Brie *see* Bridget

Briony *see* Bryony

Britt *see* Bridget

Bronwen (Celtic) the white breast
  Also Bronwyn

Brooke (Old English) at the brook

Bryony (Old English) to swell or
  grow; a plant name
  Also Breanna, Brianne, Briony

C

Caitlin (Irish) *see* Catherine

Calandra (Greek) a lark

Callista (Greek) most beautiful

Calpurnia (Latin) the name of Julius
Caesar's wife
Also Calphurnia

Camilla (Etruscan) attendant at
religious ceremonies
Also Camellia, Camila, Camille,
Kamila, Kamilla

Camira (Aboriginal) wind

Candace (Greek) glittering white or
glowing
Also Candice, Candida, Candide

Cara (Italian) dearest one
Also Carina, Carita, Kara
See also Caroline

Carina (Aboriginal) bride

Carissa (Latin) artful or skilful
Also Carisa, Chrissa

Carla (English) *see* Caroline

Carlotta *see* Charlotte

Carly (German) free woman
Also Carla, Carley, Carlita, Karla

Carma (Sanskrit) destiny

Carmel (Hebrew) vineyard or garden
Also Carmela, Carmelina,
Carmeline, Carmelita, Melina

Carmen (Spanish) songstress
Also Carmena, Carmencita, Carmia,
Carmina, Carmine, Carmita,
Charmain, Charmaine

Carol (Old French) to sing joyously
Also Carola, Carole, Caroll, Karel,
Karol
See also Caroline

Caroline (Latin) virile and strong
Feminine form of Charles (Carolus)
Also Caddie, Cara, Carla, Carlina,
Carline, Carlita, Carolina, Carolyn,
Charleen, Charlene, Karla,

Karolina, Karoline, Karoly, Karolyn,
Sharleen, Sharlene
See also Carol

Casey (Irish) courageous, brave

Casilda (Spanish) solitary one
Also Casilde, Cassilda

Casimira (Latin) bearer of peace

Cassandra (Greek) confuser of men;
one who excites love
Also Casandra, Cassandre,
Kassandra

Catarina (Italian) *see* Catherine

Catherine (Greek) pure
Also Caireen, Cairine, Caitlin,
Caitlyn, Caitrin, Caren, Carin,
Cartlin, Catalina, Catarzyna,
Cateline, Caterina, Caterine,
Catharine, Cathelina, Catherina,
Catheryn, Cathleen, Cathren,
Catlin, Catriona, Cattarina, Kaarina,
Kaatje, Kadi, Kajsa, Kalina, Kara,
Karen, Karena, Karia, Karina,
Karlinka, Karyna, Kasche, Kasia,
Kasse, Kassia, Kata, Katalin,
Katarzyna, Katchen, Kate, Katerina,
Katerine, Kateryn, Katharine,
Katherine, Kathleen, Kathryn,
Kathy, Katie, Katina, Katinka,
Katka, Katren, Katri, Katrina,
Katrine, Katti, Katura, Katushka,
Katy, Katya, Kitty
See also Kay

Cecilia (Latin) blind
Feminine form of Cecil
Also Cacilia, Cecile, Cecilie,
Cecilija, Cecily, Celia, Célie, Cicely,
Cilka, Sheelagh, Sheila, Sheilah,
Shelagh, Sileas, Sycily

Celeste (Latin) heavenly
Also Celesta, Celestina, Celestine

Celia *see* Cecilia

Celina *see* Selena

Chanda (Sanskrit) destroyer of evil

Channa (Yiddish) *see* Anne

Chantal (French) singer
Also Chantalle, Chantel, Chantelle,
Shantelle

Charis *see* Charity

Charity (Greek) love and grace
Also Charis, Charissa, Charita,
Cherry

Charlotte (French) virile and strong
Feminine form of Charles
Also Carla, Carleen, Carlina, Carlita, Carlotta, Charleen, Charlene, Charlotta, Karla, Karlotta, Lola

Charmaine (Greek) *see* Carmen

Charmian (Greek) a little joy
Also Charmion

Chen (Chinese) precious and rare

Chérie *see* Cheryl
Also Cher, Cheri

Cherry *see* Charity

Cheryl (French) dear, beloved one
Also Cher, Cheri, Chérie, Sharyl, Sherrill, Sherry, Sheryl

Chiang (Chinese) name of last queen of Yin dynasty

Chiquita (Spanish) little

Chispa (Spanish) a spark

Chloe (Greek) a young green shoot

Chloris (Greek) pale flower, fresh and blooming
Also Chloras, Clorita, Loris

Cho (Japanese) butterfly

Christabel (Greek) beautiful, bright-faced Christian
Also Christabella, Christobel, Cristabel

Christiana (Latin) *see* Christine

Christine (Greek) a Christian
Feminine form of Christian
Also Cairistine, Cairistiona, Chris, Chrissie, Chrissy, Christa, Christiana, Christiane, Christie, Christina, Christinha, Christophine, Christy, Cristin, Cristina, Cristiona, Gristin, Kirsten, Krista, Kristiana, Kristin, Kristina

Chrystal *see* Crystal

Chu (Chinese) pearl

Chun (Chinese) spring

Cilla *see* Priscilla

Cindy *see* Lucy (Lucinda)

Claire *see* Clare

Clarabelle (Latin) the clear, bright and beautiful
Also Clarabella, Claribel

Clare (Latin) clear and bright
Also Chiara, Chlaris, Claire,
Clairette, Clara, Claresta, Clareta,
Clarice, Clarinda, Clarine, Clariss,
Clarissa, Clarisse, Clarita, Clarona,
Kara, Klara, Klarika, Klarissa

Clarice (French) *see* Clare

Clarimond (Old French) bright
protector
Also Clairmond

Clarinda (Spanish) *see* Clare

Clarissa *see* Clare

Claudia (Latin) the lame
Feminine form of Claude (Claudius)
Also Claude, Claudette, Claudina,
Claudine, Clause, Klaudia

Cleine (Greek) renowned

Clematis (Greek) flower name
meaning the clinging

Clementine (Latin) the clement or
merciful
Feminine form of Clement
Also Clémence, Clemency,
Clementa, Clemente, Clementia,
Clementina, Clemenza, Cleti,
Klementina, Klementyna

Cleopatra (Greek) glory or fame
Also Cleo

Clodagh (Irish) name of a river in
Tipperary

Clorinda (Persian) renowned

Clothilda (Old German) chief or
leader's daughter
Also Clothilde, Clotilda, Klothilde

Clover (English) flower name
Also Claver

Colette (French) a small collar or
necklace
Also Coletta, Collette
See also Nicole (Nicolette)

Colleen (Irish) girl
Also Coleen, Colene

Columbine (Latin) a flower name
Also Colombe, Columba, Columbia,
Columbina

Combara (Aboriginal) tomorrow

Conception (Latin) beginning
Also Concetta

Concetta (Italian) *see* Conception

Concha (Latin) shell
  Also Conchita

Connor (Irish) high desire
  Also Conor

Constance (Latin) firm in faith
  Feminine form of Constantine
  Also Concettina, Constancia,
  Constanta, Constantia,
  Constantina, Constanz, Constanza,
  Constanzia, Custance, Konstanca,
  Konstancia, Kostancia, Kostka

Consuelo (Latin) consolation
  Also Consuela

Coolalia (Aboriginal) south wind

Cora (Greek) young maiden
  Also Corella, Corenna, Corenne,
  Coretta, Corette, Corianna, Corinna,
  Corinne, Corrie, Corry, Kora

Coral (Latin) charm
  Also Coralie, Coralina, Coraline

Cordelia (Latin) sea jewel
  Also Cordelie, Delia

Corinne *see* Cora

Cornelia (Latin) a horn

Cosette (Old German) pet lamb
  Also Cosetta

Cosima (Greek) order and harmony

Cottina (Greek) crown of wild flowers

Courtney (Old French) dweller at
  court

Cressa (Old German) water cress

Crystal (Greek) ice-clear
  Also Christel, Chrystal, Krystal

Cuc (Vietnamese) a chrysanthemum

Custance (Old English) *see* Constance

Cynthia (Greek) the moon
  Also Cinta, Cynta, Cynthie

Cyrilla (Latin) high born, lordly lady
  Feminine form of Cyril
  Also Cyrille

Cythera (Greek) from Cythera
  Also Cytheria

Czenzi (Hungarian) increasing

D

Dacia (Greek) an ancient country north of the Danube
Also Dachia

Dagmar (Danish) glory of the Danes
Also Dagmara

Dahlia (Latin) flower name, of the valley

Daisy (Old English) day's eye, flower name

Dai-Tai (Chinese) spring

Dale (Old English) valley
Also Dayle

Dalila (African) gentle

Dallas (Old Irish) the skilled and wise

Damaris (Greek) tame or gentle
Also Damara

Damaspla (Persian) horse tamer

Damayanti (Sanskrit) pearl of girls

Dana *see* Danica

Danella *see* Daniela

Danette (Old German) little mistress
Also Danete, Danetta

Danica (Norse) the morning star
Also Dahna, Dana, Danah, Dayna

Daniela (Hebrew) God is my judge
Feminine form of Daniel
Also Danella, Danete, Danetta, Danette, Daniell, Danielle, Danila, Danita, Danka, Dannetej, Danya, Danye

Danielle (French) *see* Daniela

Daphne (Greek) bay or laurel, a flower name
Also Daphna

Dara (Hebrew) charity, compassion and wisdom
Also Darra

Darcle (Celtic) dark

Daria (Persian) queenly
Also Darice, Darya

Darlene (Old English) little darling
Also Darelle, Darleen

Davida *see* Davina

Davina (Scottish) beloved; loved by
God
Feminine form of David
Also Dainia, Davida, Davita, Vida,
Vidette, Vita

Dawn (Old English) break of day
See also Aurora

Dea (Latin) goddess

Dealva (Latin) white

Deanna *see* Diana

Deborah (Hebrew) the bee, implying
wisdom and eloquence
Also Deberah, Debora, Debra, Devora

Decima (Latin) the tenth child

Deirdre (Old Irish) sorrowing or
broken-hearted

Delia (Greek) moon goddess
Also Delena
See also Cordelia

Delilah (Hebrew) the gentle
temptress, desire
Also Lila

Della (Old German) noble

Delora (Latin) from the seashore
Also Ellora

Delores *see* Dolores

Delvine (Greek) of Delphi
Also Delfina, Delfine, Delphine

Denise (French) after the god
of wine, Dionysos
Feminine form of Dennis
(Dionysos)
Also Denice, Denys, Dione,
Dionetta, Dionette, Dionis, Dionne,
Dionycia, Dionysia

Desdemona (Greek) misery

Désirée (French) desired one
Also Desiderata, Desiderius

Desmia (Latin) a beautiful butterfly

Desolin (Old French) left alone

Deva (Sanskrit) divine shining light
Also Devi

Devona (Old English) of Devon

Diana (Latin) name of the goddess
of the moon
Also Deana, Deane, Deanna,
Deanne, Diahann, Diane, Dianna,
Dyan, Dyana, Dyane, Dyann

Dido (Greek) teacher

Diella (Latin) worshipper of God

Dilys (Welsh) genuine, perfect
Also Delys

Dinah (Hebrew) the judged,
vindicated
Also Dina, Dyna

Dione (Greek) *see* Denise

Dionysia *see* Denise

Dolly (Old English) a doll

Dolores (Spanish) lady of sorrow
Also Delora, Delores, Deloris,
Delorita, Doloritas, Dolour, Lola,
Lolita

Dominique (French) belonging to
the Lord
Feminine form of Dominic
Also Domeneca, Domenica,

Dominga, Domini, Dominica,
Dominik

Donalee (Celtic) sheltered gift

Doncella (Latin) a damsel

Dongala (Old Irish) dark maiden

Donna (Italian) refined lady
Also Dona

Dora *see* Dorothy

Dorcas (Greek) gazelle
Also Dorcea, Dorcia

Doreen (French) the golden or
gilded
Also Doireen, Dorene, Dori, Dorie,
Dorine, Dory

Dorinda (Greek) the beautiful; of the
ocean
Also Dorea, Doria, Dorie, Doris,
Dorise, Dorita, Dorris

Doris *see* Dorinda

Dorothy (Greek) gift of God
Also Darata, Darinka, Diorbhail,
Dora, Dorchen, Dore, Doretta,
Dorosia, Dorota, Dorotea, Doroteja,
Dorothea, Dorothee, Dorothi,

Dorotka, Dortha, Dorthea, Dorthy, Thea, Theodora
See also Theodora

Dousabel (Old English) sweet and fair
Also Dowsabel
See also Dulcie

Drusilla (Latin) the strong one

Dulcie (Latin) sweet and charming
Diminutive form of Dulcinea
Also Delcine, Dulce, Dulcea, Dulcia, Dulciana, Dulcibella, Dulcibelle, Dulcinea, Dulcinia, Dulcyna

Duvessa (Irish) dark beauty

Dyan *see* Diana

Dymphna (Irish) a poet

Dysis (Greek) the sunset

E

Eartha (Old English) of the earth
  Also Ertha

Easter (Greek) child born at Eastertide

Ebba (Old English) tide

Eden (Hebrew) pleasure or place of pleasure

Edith (Old English) rich, prosperous and happy
  Also Eadith, Eaditha, Eda, Edda, Eddeva, Ede, Edetta, Edeva, Edina, Edita, Editha, Edithe, Edyth, Edytha, Edythe

Edmonda (Old English) prosperous protector
  Feminine form of Edmund
  Also Edmee

Edna (Hebrew) rejuvenation

Edrena (Old English) prosperous ruler
  Also Edrea, Edris

Edwina (Old English) rich or happy friend

Feminine form of Edwin
  Also Edwinna

Eereena (Greek) messenger of peace

Effie *see* Euphemia

Eileen (Irish) *see* Helen

Eithne *see* Aithne

Elaine (French) *see* Helen

Elana (Greek) *see* Helen

Elcy (Old German) noble cheer

Eleanor (Provencal) *see* Helen

Electra (Greek) the brilliant one

Elfleda (Old English) noble, beautiful; elf strength
  Also Ethelfleda

Elfrida (Old German) wise and peaceful; elfin
  Also Elfreda, Elfredah

Elia (Hebrew) God's own

Elisa (German) *see* Elizabeth

Elissa (Phoenician) *see* Elizabeth

Eliza (English) *see* Elizabeth

Elizabeth (Hebrew) oath of God
Also Alzbieta, Alzebeta, Belita,
Bess, Besse, Bessie, Bessy, Beth,
Betje, Betsy, Bette, Betti, Bettina,
Bettisa, Betty, Betuska, Ealasaid,
Eilis, Elas, Elen, Elined, Elinud,
Elisa, Elisabet, Elisabeth,
Elisabetta, Elise, Elissa, Eliza, Ellen,
Ellyn, Elsabet, Elsbetchen, Elsbeth,
Else, Elsie, Elspeth, Elyssa, Elze,
Erzebet, Eylse, Isabeau, Isabel,
Isabella, Isabelle, Iseabal, Isobel,
Liese, Liesel, Liesl, Lilibet, Lisa,
Lisabetta, Lisabette, Lisette, Liza,
Lizabeth, Lizaveta, Lizette,
Yelisaveta, Ysabel

Ella (Old English) beautiful fairy
maiden
See also Helen

Ellen *see* Helen

Ellora (Greek) happy

Elmira (Old English) of noble fame
See also Almira

Eloise (Old German) *see* Louise

Elsa (Old German) *see* Ailsa

Elsie *see* Elizabeth

Elspeth (Scottish) *see* Elizabeth

Elva (Old German) elfin

Elvira (Latin) white
Also Albina, Albinia, Alvira, Elvire

Elysia (Greek) pleasure and happiness

Emerant (Old German) the emerald

Emily (English) industrious
Also Aimil, Amala, Amalea, Amalia,
Amalie, Amelia, Amelie, Amelija,
Amelina, Amelinda, Ameline,
Amelita, Amilia, Emalia, Emelda,
Emelia, Emeline, Emera, Emilia,
Emiliana, Emilie, Emilija, Emlyn,
Emmarine, Emmelina, Emmeline

Emma (Old German) whole or
universal
Also Emme, Emmot, Imma
See also Emily (Emmeline)

Emmanuella (French) God is with us
Feminine form of Emmanuel
See also Manuela

Emmeline *see* Emily

Emogene *see* Imogen

Ena (Gaelic) ardent or fiery

Enid (Celtic) purity of the soul
Also Enaid

Enola (North American Indian) alone

Eolande (Greek) born of the wind

Epifania *see* Tiffany

Eranthe (Greek) alternative name for
the herb chamomile

Erica (Old Norse) powerful ruler
Feminine form of Eric
Also Erika

Erin (Old Irish) girl
Also Erina, Erine, Erinna, Erinne

Erma *See* Irma

Ermina (Latin) lordly

Ernestine (Old German) earnest
Feminine form of Ernest
Also Erna, Ernesta, Ernestina,
Ernestyna

Ersilia (Gaelic) of Irish extraction

Esmé *see* Amy

Esmerelda (Spanish) jewel, emerald
Also Emerald, Esma, Esmeralda,
Esmerolda

Esperance (French) hope

Essie *see* Esther

Estelle (French) *see* Esther

Esther (Persian) a star
Also Eister, Essie, Estella, Estelle,
Estelline, Ester, Estrelda, Estrella,
Estrellita, Hester, Hestera, Hesther,
Hestia, Hetty, Stella, Stelle

Ethel (Old English) noble maiden
Also Ethelda, Etheldrid, Ethelind,
Ethelinda, Etheline, Ethelyn, Ethyle

Etta *see* Henrietta

Ettienette *see* Stephanie

Eucaria (Italian) ready hand, dextrous
Also Euchira

Eugenia (Greek) nobility, excellence
Feminine form of Eugene
Also Eugenie, Genie

Eulalia (Greek) of fair speech
Also Eulalie

Eunice (Greek) happy victory

Euphemia (Greek) of good repute
Also Effie, Eufamie, Eufemia,
Euphemiah, Euphemie, Euthemie,
Phemia

Euphrasia (Greek) generous and
joyful
Also Eufrazya, Euphrazya

Eustacia (Greek) fruitful
Feminine form of Eustace
Also Eustachia, Eustacie, Stacie,
Stacy

Evangeline (French) happy
messenger

Eve (Hebrew) life-giving
Also Aoiffe, Eeva, Eva, Evita, Evva

Evelyn (Old German) ancestor, little
Eve
Also Evaleen, Evalina, Eveleen,
Evelina, Eveline, Evlyn

Evonne *see* Yvonne

F

Fabia (Latin) ancient Roman family name derived from bean grower Feminine form of Fabian
Also Fabian, Fabiana, Fabienne, Fabiola, Fabyan

Faiga (Old English) beautiful

Faine (Old English) joyous
Also Faina, Fayna, Fayne

Fairlee (Old English) beautiful forest
Also Fairlie

Faith (Latin) to trust
Also Fae, Fay, Faye

Fanny *see* Frances

Far (Chinese) flower

Fay (Old French) *see* Faith

Fayar (Polynesian) dawn

Fayme (Old English) fame
Also Fameuse

Fayola (African) walks with honour

Fedora *see* Theodora

Felicity (Latin) happy
Feminine form of Felix
Also Felice, Felicia, Felicianna, Felicidad, Felicie, Felicija, Felicita, Felicitas, Felicite, Felicitia, Felis, Felise

Fenella (Gaelic) *see* Fiona

Fern (Old English) a wing or feather
Also Ferna, Fernas

Fidella (Latin) faithful
Feminine form of Fidel
Also Fedellas, Fidela, Fidelia, Fidelle, Fidellia, Fidellis

Fifine (Hebrew) addition
Also Fifi

Finella (Celtic) *see* Fiona

Fiona (Gaelic) fair one or white one
Also Fenella, Fia, Finella, Finola, Finvola, Fionna, Fionnuala, Fionnula, Fionola, Fynvola, Phia, Phio, Phiona, Phionna

Fiorella *see* Florence

Flavia (Latin) blonde or golden-
haired
Also Flavie

Fleur (French) flower
Also Fleurette

Flora (Latin) name of the goddess of
flowers

Florence (Latin) flowering,
flourishing
Also Fiora, Fiorella, Fiorenza,
Firenze, Flora, Flore, Florene,
Florentia, Florentina, Florentine,
Florentyna, Florenz, Florette,
Floria, Florice, Florinda, Florine,
Floris

Frances (Latin) free; from France
Feminine form of Francis

Also Fania, Fanny, Fanya, Fraka,
Fran, Franca, Francelia, Francella,
Francesca, Franchon, Francine,
Francisca, Francisquita, Francoise,
Francyne, Franka, Franzchen,
Franziska, Frasquita

Freda (German) peaceful
Also Frieda, Frida

Frederika (German) peaceful ruler
Feminine form of Frederick
Also Farica, Fiedricke, Frederica,
Fredericka, Frederique, Fredrica,
Fredrika, Frenderica, Fridrada

Freya (Old Norse) name of the
goddess of love and beauty
Also Frea, Freyja

Fuiju (Japanese) winter

Fung (Chinese) bird

G

Gabrielle (Hebrew) woman of God
Also Gabella, Gable, Gabriel,
Gabriela, Gabriella, Gabrilla,
Gabrioletta, Gabryela, Gavilla, Gavra

Gaea (Greek) of the earth
Also Gaia

Gaeta (Sanskrit) holy
Also Geeta, Gita

Gai (Old French) lively
Also Gay, Gaye

Gail (Old English) to sing
Also Gailene, Gale, Gayle, Gaylene
See also Abigail

Galatea (Greek) milk-white

Garda (Old German) guarded or
prepared
Also Gardas, Gardda, Garde, Gardia
See also Gertrude

Gay *see* Gai

Gayle *see* Gail

Gaynor *see* Genevieve

Gemma (Latin) precious stone or
trinket
Also Gemmie, Gemsie, Jemma

Genevieve (Celtic) white wave
Also Ganor, Gaynor, Geneva,
Genevieffa, Genevion, Genevra,
Gennifer, Genoveva, Genowefa,
Ginette, Ginevra, Ginevre, Jenavive,
Jennavah, Jennifer, Vanora
See also Guinevere, Gwendolen

Genie *see* Eugenia

Gentian (Greek) flower name

Georgina (Greek) tiller of the soil
Feminine form of George
Also Georgana, Georgene,
Georgetta, Georgette, Georgia,
Georgiana, Georgienne, Georgine,
Gina, Girogia

Geraldine (Old German) spear and
rule
Feminine form of Gerald
Also Geralda, Geraldina, Gerardine,
Gerelda, Gerhardine, Gerlinda,
Giralda, Jeraldine

Gerda (Norse) *see* Gertrude

Geremia *see* Jeremia

Germaine (French) of Germany
Also Germain

Gertrude (Old German) the strong
spear-maiden
Also Geltruda, Gerda, Gerde,
Gerite, Gerta, Gertrud, Gertrudis,
Gerty, Kerttu, Truda, Trude, Trudi,
Trudy

Gigi *see* Gilberta

Gilberta (Old German) bright pledge
Feminine form of Gilbert
Also Gigi, Gilberte, Gilbertina,
Gilbertine, Wilba, Wilbera, Wilberta

Gilda (Old English) the gilded or
golden

Gillian (Latin) young nestling
Also Gileta, Giliana, Giliane, Gill,
Gilliet, Gilliette, Jiliette, Jill, Jillian,
Jilliana, Jillianne, Jilliette

Gina *see* Georgina

Giselle (Old German) pledge
Also Gisela, Giselda, Gisele, Gisella,
Gizela

Githa (Norse) war

Gladys (Latin) a sword
Also Gladine, Gladusa, Gladuse,
Gwladys

Glenna (Celtic) of the glen or valley
Feminine form of Glen
Also Glenda, Glendene, Glendora,
Glenn, Glennie, Glennis, Glenyss,
Glynis

Gloria (Latin) glory
Also Gloriana, Gloriane

Glynis *see* Glenna

Godiva (Old English) God's gift

Goldie (Old English) pure gold
Also Golda, Goldea, Goldye, Zlota

Grace (Latin) the loved, favoured,
honoured
Also Engracia, Giorsal, Graca,
Graciana, Gracie, Gracienne,
Graciosa, Gracye, Gratia, Gratiana,
Grazia, Graziella, Grazielle,
Graziosa, Grecia, Gricia

Gracilia (Latin) slender

Greta (German) *see* Margaret

Gretchen (German) *see* Margaret

Griselda (Old German) grey battle-maid
Also Chriselda, Grisel, Griseldis, Grishilda, Grishilde, Grissell, Grizel, Grizelda, Grizzel, Selda, Zelda

Gudrid (Old Norse) divine passion
Also Gudron, Gudrun, Gudruna, Guthrun

Guida (Italian) a guide
Feminine form of Guy
Also Guietta, Guillena

Guilia *see* Julia

Guinevere (Celtic) white phantom
Also Genevra, Ginevra, Guenevere, Guinievre
See also Genevieve, Gwendolen

Gunhild (Old German) brave warrior-maid
Also Gunhilda, Gunhilde

Gwenda *see* Gwendolin

Gwendolen (Welsh) the white one
Also Guendolen, Gwen, Gwenda, Gwendaline, Gwendolin, Gwendoline, Gwendolyn, Gwenn,
See also Genevieve, Guinevere

Gwynne *see* Gwyneth

Gwyneth (Welsh) blessed
Also Gwenith, Gwyn, Gwynne, Venetia

H

Hadassah (Hebrew) a star
   See also Esther

Haidee (Greek) modest, caressed
   Also Haida, Haido, Haydee

Halina *see* Helen

Halona (North American Indian)
   happy fortune
   Also Halonna

Hana (Japanese) flower

Hannah (Hebrew) *see* Anne

Harriet (English) home ruler
   Feminine form of Harold (Harry)
   Also Arriet, Harriett, Harrietta,
   Harriette, Harriot, Hatty
   See also Henrietta

Haru (Japanese) spring

Hasina (African) good

Hatty *see* Harriet

Hayley (Old English) hay maiden
   Also Haylea, Haylee

Hazel (Old English) the hazel tree

Heather (Scottish) flower of the
   moors

Hebe (Greek) youth

Hedda (Old German) war or strife
   Also Avice, Avise, Havoise, Heda,
   Hedwig, Hedwiga
   See also Heidi

Heidi (German) battle-maid
   Also Heide, Heidy, Hidie

Helen (Greek) bright one
   Feminine form of Helenas
   Also Aileen, Ailienor, Alaine,
   Alaune, Alena, Alene, Alienor,
   Aline, Eileen, Eilene, Eilleen, Elain,
   Elaine, Elana, Elayne, Eleanor,
   Eleanora, Eleanore, Eleen, Elena,
   Elene, Elenor, Elenore, Eleonore,
   Elidh, Elini, Elinor, Elinore, Elionor,
   Ellen, Ellene, Ellenis, Ellette, Ellie,
   Ellin, Ellyn, Elmor, Elna, Elnore,

Elyn, Gailina, Galena, Galina,
Halina, Helaine, Helena, Helene,
Helenka, Helenora, Hellene, Ileana,
Ilene, Illene, Ilona, Jelena, Jeleta,
Jellica, Laine, Lana, Lani, Leanor,
Lena, Lenia, Lenke, Lenni, Lennie,
Lenor, Lenore, Leonora, Leonore,
Leora, Lora, Lorene, Lorine,
Narelle, Nell, Nella, Nellette,
Nelliana, Nellie, Nillette, Nora,
Norah, Norelle, Yelena

Helga (Old Norse) the holy
Feminine form of Helgi
Also Elga, Olga

Helise (Greek) of the Elysian fields
Also Helice

Heloise (French) *see* Louise

Henrietta (Old German) home ruler
Feminine form of Henry
Also Eiric, Enrica, Enrichetta,
Enrieta, Enrika, Enriqueta,
Enriquette, Etta, Hattie, Hendrica,
Hendrika, Henka, Henrieta,
Henriette, Henrika, Henrike,
Henriqueta, Jettchen, Jindriska,
Nettie
See also Harriet, Yetta

Hepzibah (Hebrew) my delight is in
her
Also Hephzibah, Hephzipa,
Hepsiba, Hepsibah, Hepsy, Hepza,
Hebzi, Hebzibeth, Zipah

Hera (Greek) queen of the gods and
protector of women

Hermione [Her-my-o-nee] (Greek)
noble
Feminine form of Hermes
Also Hermanda, Hermandine,
Hermia, Hermine, Herminia, Irma

Hester *see* Esther

Hilary (Greek) cheerful and merry
Also Hilar, Hilaria, Hillari

Hilda (Old English) battle
Also Hilde, Hildie, Hiltrud, Hylda,
Ilda, Ilde

Hildegarde (Old German) protecting
battle-maid
Also Hildegard, Hildagarde,
Hildegard
See also Hilda

Hippolyta (Greek) liberator of horses
Feminine form of Hippolytus

Hiroko (Japanese) generous

Holly (Old English) holy
 Also Hollie

Honey (Old English) sweet one

Hong (Chinese) pink

Honora (Latin) reputation for beauty
 Also Annora, Honora, Honoria,
 Nora, Norah, Onora, Onoria

Hope (Old English) to hope or
 cherish
 See also Nadia

Hortense (Latin) a lady gardener
 Also Hortencia, Hortensa,
 Hortensia, Hortenzia, Ortensa,
 Ortensia

Hoshi (Japanese) star

Howin (Chinese) a loyal swallow

Hua (Chinese) flower, blossom

Hulda (Norse) muffled or covered

Huli (Chinese) fox spirit

Hyacinth (Greek) hyacinth flower or
 colour purple
 Also Chinta, Giacinta, Hyacintha,
 Hyacinthia, Hyacinthies, Jacinda,
 Jacinta, Jacintha, Jacinthe, Jacyne

Hypatia (Greek) superior

I

Ianthe (Greek) *see* Violet

Ida (Old German) happy
  Also Idaka, Idalia, Idda, Idetta, Idette

Idala (Hebrew) one who goes softly

Idona (Old Norse) name of the
  goddess of spring
  Also Edony, Idonea, Idonia

Ignacia (Latin) ardent; fiery
  Feminine form of Ignatius
  Also Igna, Ignazia, Ignezia, Iniga

Ila (French) isle

Ilka (Scottish) each and every one
  (Slavic) flattering
  Also Milka

Ilona (Hungarian) *see* Helen

Ilsa *see* Alisa

Imelda *see* Imogen

Imogen (Latin) image of her mother
  Also Emogene, Imagina, Imelda,
  Imogene, Imogine, Imojean

Ina (Filipino) mother

Inari (Japanese) keeper of rice

Indira (Sanskrit) an Indian goddess

Indra (Hindustani) the thunder
  Also Indred

Inez (Spanish) *see* Agnes

Ingrid (Old Norse) the daughter of
  the great hero Ing
  Also Inga, Ingar, Inge, Ingeberg,
  Inger, Ingria, Ingrida, Ingunna

Inocenta (Italian) innocent
  Also Chencho, Innocenty

Iola (Greek) dawn cloud
  Also Iole

Iolanthe (Greek) *see* Violet

Irene (Greek) peace
  Also Arina, Eereenia, Eirena,
  Eirene, Erena, Irena, Irenka, Irina

Iris (Greek) the rainbow

Irma (Old German) strong
(Latin) noble person
Also Erma, Ermina, Erminia, Irme,
Irmina, Irmine
See also Hermione

Iruka (African) the future is supreme

Isa (Old German) iron-like

Isadora (Greek) the gift of Isis
Feminine form of Isidore
Also Dora, Isadore, Isidora

Ismenia (Greek) learned
Also Ismena

Isobel (Spanish) *see* Elizabeth

Isolda (Old German) ice rule
Also Isolde

Ita (Gaelic) desire for truth

Ivy (Old English) ivy vine
Also Ivana, Ive, Ivis

J

Jacinta *see* Hyacinth

Jacobina (Scottish) *see* Jacqueline

Jacqueline (French) the supplanter
Feminine form of Jacob (Jacques)
Also Jacalyn, Jacina, Jackelyn,
Jacoba, Jacobee, Jacobella,
Jacobina, Jacobine, Jacomina,
Jacovina, Jacquelina, Jacquelyn,
Jacquenella, Jacquenetta,
Jacquenette, Jacquetta, Jacquette,
Jacqui, Jakolin, Jakolina, Zakolina
See also Jamesina

Jade (Chinese) love

Jama (Sanskrit) daughter

Jamesina (Scottish) the supplanter
Feminine form of Jacob (James)
Also Jesma
See also Jacqueline

Jamila (African) beautiful

Jan *see* Jane

Jana *see* Jane

Jane (Hebrew) God is gracious
Feminine form of John
Also Gian, Gianina, Gianna, Giovanna,
Ivanka, Jan, Jana, Janeen, Janeis,
Janel, Janella, Janelle, Janelyn,
Janet, Janeta, Janeth, Janetta,
Janette, Janica, Janice, Janie, Janina,
Janine, Janis, Janka, Jann, Janna,
Jannah, Janne, Jasia, Jayne, Jean,
Jeanette, Jeanine, Jeanne, Jehanne,
Jenet, Jenka, Jennetta, Jennette,
Jhone, Joan, Joana, Joanie, Joanna,
Joanne, Johanna, Jone, Joni, Jonie,
Jonita, Jovanna, Juana, Juanita,
Seonaid, Shane, Shauna, Sheena,
Sheenah, Sheenaugh, Shena, Shene,
Shona, Sian, Sine, Sinead, Siobhan,
Zane, Zaneta

Janelle *see* Jane

Janice *see* Jane

Janina (Sanskrit) the kind
See also Jane

Jarita (Hindustani) the bird
Also Arita, Gerita, Jerita, Rita

Jarvia (Old German) sharp as a spear
Feminine form of Jarvis

Jasmine (Persian) the jasmine flower
Also Jamina, Jasmin, Jasmina,
Jassamine, Jessamine, Jessamy,
Jessamyn, Yasmin, Yasmine

Javana (Sanskrit) swift, fleet

Jayne *see* Jane

Jean (Scottish) *see* Jane

Jeanette (French) *see* Jane

Jemima (Hebrew) the dove, the
symbol of peace
Also Jemena, Jemimah, Jemina,
Jeminah, Jeminine

Jemma *see* Gemma

Jennifer (English) *see* Genevieve

Jeremia (Hebrew) the Lord's exalted
Feminine form of Jeremiah
Also Geremia

Jessamine (French) *see* Jasmine

Jessica (Hebrew) God's grace; he
beholds
Feminine form of Jesse

Also Jessalyn, Jesseline, Jessie,
Jessika, Jesslyn

Jezebel (Hebrew) devotee of Baal, a
false god

Jillian *see* Gillian

Joan *see* Jane

Joanna *see* Jane

Jocasta (Greek) queen of Thebes

Jocelyn (Latin) just one
Also Giusta, Giustina, Jocelin,
Joceline, Jodoca, Joscelind,
Josceline, Joscely, Joscelyn, Joslin,
Josselyn, Joycelin

Jocosa (Latin) playful

Jodie *see* Judith

Johanna *see* Jane

Joletta (Latin) *see* Violet

Jolie (French) pretty

Josephine (French) increaser
Feminine form of Joseph
Also Giuseppina, Iosefini, Josefa,

Josefina, Josepha, Josephe, Josephie,
Josephina, Josette, Jozia, Jozka,
Juozapina, Pepina, Pepita

Joy (Latin) to rejoice
Also Joice, Joyan, Joyce, Joye,
Joyons

Joyce *see* Joy

Juanita (Spanish) *see* Jane

Judith (Hebrew) woman of Judea; a
jewess
Also Giuditta, Iudita, Jodi, Jodie,
Jody, Judi, Judie, Judita, Juditha,
Judithe, Judy, Jutha, Jutta, Jytte,
Yudif

Julia (Latin) youthful one
Feminine form of Julian
Also Guilia, Guiliana, Guilietta, Ioula,

Iulia, Joletta, Juliana, Juliane,
Julianne, Julie, Julienne, Juliet,
Julieta, Julietta, Juliette, Julija,
Julina, Juline, Julita, Julyan, Zulliette

Jun (Chinese) truth

June (Latin) born in the month of
June
Also Jeno, Juna, Junella, Juneth,
Junette, Junia, Junna, Junno, Juno

Justine (French) the just
Feminine form of Justin
Also Guistina, Justa, Justicia,
Justina, Justinka, Yustyna

Juventia (Latin) name of the
goddess of youth

K

Kachina (North American Indian) sacred dancer

Kama (Sanskrit) love

Kamala (Sanskrit) lotus

Kamania (African) like the moon

Kameka (Japanese) long-lived

Kane (Japanese) golden

Karen (Danish) *see* Catherine

Karma (Sanskrit) destiny
  Also Carma

Karoline *see* Caroline

Kasia (Polish) *see* Catherine

Kate *see* Catherine

Katherine *see* Catherine

Kathleen *see* Catherine

Katinka (Russian) *see* Catherine

Katrina *see* Catherine

Kay (Greek) to rejoice
  Also Kaya, Kaye, Kaylene
  See also Catherine (Katherine)

Keely (Gaelic) the beautiful one
  Also Keele, Keelie

Keiko (Japanese) beloved, adored

Kelly (Gaelic) warrior-maid

Kelsey (Old Norse) from the island

Kendra (Old English) knowing or understanding
  Also Kenna

Kerry (Celtic) the dark
  Also Keri, Kerrie

Ketura (Hebrew) incense, fragrance
  Also Keturah

Kezia (Hebrew) the cassia tree
  Also Kazia, Kesi, Kesia, Kesiah, Ketsy, Kezi, Kitsy

Kiki (Egyptian) the castor plant

Kim (English) chief or ruler
 Also Kym
 See also Kimberley

Kimberley (English) from the royal
 meadow
 Also Kimberly

Kineta (Greek) active

Kira (Persian) sun

Kiri (Maori) tree bark
 Also Kirilees, Kirilly, Kirri

Kirsten (Scottish) *see* Christine

Kitty *see* Catherine

Kiyoko (Japanese) clear

Klara (German) *see* Clare

Kora *see* Cora

Krishna (Sanskrit) dark or black

Kuki (Japanese) snow

Kuni (Japanese) country born

Kwai (Chinese) fragrance of a rose

Kylie (Aboriginal) boomerang

Kyna (Welsh) wise and mighty
 Feminine form of Conan (Kynan)

L

Laelia (Hebrew) devoted to the Lord
Also Laila, Lela, Lelah, Lelia, Lelie

Lais (Greek) rejoice
Also Laise

Lakshmi (Sanskrit) success and beauty

Lala (Slavic) tulip

Lalage (Greek) babble

Lalla (Scottish) of the lowlands

Lana *see* Alana

Lani (Maori) flower

Lara (Latin) famous, shining
Also Larah, Larentia, Laretta

Larissa (Greek) cheerful one

Laura (Latin) crowned with laurel
Feminine form of Laurence
Also Lari, Laurana, Lauranna,
Laure, Laureen, Laurel, Lauren,
Laurena, Laurencia, Laurene,
Laurentia, Laurentina, Lauretta,
Laurette, Laurinda, Lora, Loralie,
Lore, Loree, Lorelie, Lorelle, Loren,
Lorena, Lorenza, Loretta, Lorette,
Lori, Lorinda, Lorine, Loris, Lorita,
Lorna, Lorne, Lorrie, Loure,
Lourane, Lourena

Laurel *see* Laura

Lauren *see* Laura

Lavinia (Latin) woman of Latium
Also Laletta

Layla (African) born at night

Lea (English) the lea or grassland
Also Leigh

Leah (Hebrew) the weary one

Leala (Old French) faithful

Leanne *combination* of Lee and Anne
See also Liana

Lee (Chinese) plum

Leigh *see* Lea

Leila (Persian) dark, oriental beauty

Leilani (Hawaiian) heavenly blossom
Also Lillani, Lullani

Lena *see* Helen

Leonie (Latin) the lion
Feminine form of Leo
Also Leocadia, Leola, Leona,
Leonarda, Leone, Leonella,
Leonelle, Leoni, Leonia, Leonina,
Leonine, Leontine, Leontyne

Leonora *see* Helen (Eleanor)

Lesley (Celtic) from the grey
stronghold
Feminine form of Leslie
Also Leslee, Lesleigh

Letitia (Latin) gladness
Also Laetitia, Lece, Leda, Leetice,
Leticia, Letizia, Letta, Lettice

Lettice (English) *see* Letitia

Lewanna (Hebrew) as pure as the
white moon

Lian (Chinese) graceful willow

Liana (French) to bind
See also Leanne

Lida (Slavonic) loved by all people

Liesl (German) *see* Elizabeth

Lila *see* Delilah

Lilac (Persian) flower name

Lilith (Assyrian) storm demon

Lillian (Latin) flower name, lily
Also Lela, Lelah, Lelia, Lila, Lilah,
Lili, Lilia, Lilian, Liliana, Liliane,
Lilianna, Liliarna, Lilias, Lilicia,
Lilja, Liljana, Lillah, Lillis, Lily, Lilyan

Linda (Old German) wise serpent
Also Linde, Lindi, Lindie, Lindy,
Lynd, Lynda, Lynn, Lynne
See also Belinda, Melinda

Linette *see* Lynette

Lisa *see* Elizabeth

Lisette *see* Elizabeth

Lisle (Old English) of the island

Lissabelle (Latin) beautiful honey bee

Liza *see* Elizabeth

Lois (Greek) free to please

Lola (Spanish) *see* Charlotte, Dolores

Lorelei (German) lurer to the rock

Loretta *see* Laura

Lori *see* Laura

Loris *see* Chloris

Lorna (Celtic) name of a goddess of the moors
See also Laura

Lorraine (French) famous in battle
Also Laraine, Loraine

Louise (Latin) to hear and to fight
Feminine form of Lewis (Louis)
Also Aloisa, Aloisia, Aloyse, Eloisa, Eloise, Heloisa, Heloise, Labhaoise, Loise, Louisa, Louisetta, Louisette, Lovisa, Loyce, Ludvika, Luigia, Luisa, Luise, Lujza, Lujzka, Lula

Lucasta *see* Lucy

Lucia (Italian) *see* Lucy

Lucinda *see* Lucy

Lucretia [Loo-kreshia] (Latin) riches or reward
Feminine form of Lucretius

Also Lucrece, Lucrecia, Lucree, Lucrezia

Lucy (Latin) light
Also Cindy, Lucasta, Lucette, Lucia, Luciana, Lucida, Lucie, Lucienne, Lucila, Lucile, Lucilia, Lucilla, Lucille, Lucina, Lucinda, Lucza, Luighseach, Luisadh, Luz, Luzette, Luzie, Luzija, Luzinde

Luella (Old English) famous elf
Also Llewella, Louella, Loulle, Lovella, Luelle

Lulabel (Old German) beautiful war hero

Lulu (African) precious pearl

Lurline (Old German) the alluring

Lycia *see* Alice

Lydia (Greek) woman of Lydia, a rich trading country in ancient Asia Minor
Also Lidia, Lidie, Lidika, Lydie

Lynda *see* Linda

Lyndal (Old English) in the dale
Also Lindall

Lyndsay (Old English) linden tree
Also Lyndsey

Lynette (Latin) the flax
Also Eluned, Linetta, Linette,
Lyneth, Lynetta, Lynette, Lynn

Lynn *see* Linda, Lynette

Lysandra (Greek) liberator

M

Mab (Celtic) joy

Mabel (Latin) lovable
Also Amabel, Amabella, Annabel,
Annabella, Arrabel, Arrabella,
Mabella, Mabelle, Mabilia, Mabilla,
Mable, Maible, Mas, Maybelle

Madeline (Hebrew) woman of
Magdala in Galilee
Also Madalene, Madaline, Madalon,
Madalyn, Maddalena, Maddie,
Madel, Madelaine, Madeleine,
Madelena, Madelene, Madelina,
Madella, Madelle, Madelon,
Madlen, Madlena, Madlin, Madlyn,
Mady, Magda, Magdala, Magdalen,
Magdalena, Magdalene, Magdaline,
Magdolna, Maighdlin, Malena,
Malina, Marlane, Marlene, Marleen,
Marlina, Marline

Madge *see* Margaret

Madhura (Sanskrit) charming,
delightful

Maeve (Celtic) intoxicating joy
Also Mave, Meave

Magda (German) *see* Madeline

Magnolia (Latin) flower name

Mahlah (Hebrew) mild

Maida (Old English) the maiden
Also Maidel, Maidie, Mayda,
Mayde, Maydena

Maire (Irish) *see* Mary

Maisie (Scottish) *see* Margaret

Makaira (Japanese) happy

Mali *see* Malvina

Malina (Danish) *see* Madeline

Malvina (Old German) smooth brow
Feminine form of Melvin
Also Maleena, Mali, Malin, Mallie,
Mallina, Malva, Malvinia, Mellie,
Melvina, Melvine, Molina

Mame *see* Mary

Manuela (Spanish) God with us
Feminine form of Manuel
Also Manella, Mannuela, Manuelita,
Uella
See also Emmanuella

Marah *see* Mary

Marcella *see* Marcia

Marcia (Latin) belonging to Mars,
the god of war
Feminine form of Mark
Also Marcela, Marcelia, Marcelina,
Marcelinda, Marceline, Marcella,
Marcelle, Marcellina, Marcelline,
Marcerita, Marcheta, Marchita,
Marciana, Marcie, Marcille,
Marcine, Marcite, Marka, Marquita,
Marsha

Mardi (French) Tuesday

Margaret (Latin) pearl
Also Greta, Gretchen, Gretel,
Madge, Madlinka, Mairghread,
Maisie, Marcail, Margareta,
Margarete, Margaretha,
Margaretta, Margarida, Margarita,
Margaux, Margelo, Margery,
Marget, Margette, Margharita,
Margherethe, Margherita, Margory,
Margot, Margred, Margret,
Marguerita, Marguerite, Marjorie,

Marjory, Marret, May, Maygan,
Meadleh, Meagan, Meaghan, Meg,
Megan, Meghann, Meta, Peg, Peggy,
See also Rita

Margery (English) *see* Margaret

Margherita (Spanish) *see* Margaret
and Rita

Margita (Sanskrit) sought after

Margot (French) *see* Margaret

Maria (Latin) *see* Mary

Marian *see* Mary

Maribelle *combination* of Mary and
Belle
Also Marabelle, Maribel, Maribella,
Marybelle

Marie (French) *see* Mary

Marietta (American) *see* Mary

Marigold (English) flower name

Marika (Spanish) *see* Mary

Marilyn (American) *see* Mary

Marina (Latin) of the sea
  Also Mareena, Marisa

Marion (English) *see* Mary

Marjorie *see* Margaret

Marlene (Hebrew) the elevated
  See also Madeline

Marsha *see* Marcia

Martha (Aramaic) head of the
  household
  Also Marta, Martel, Martella,
  Marthe, Marthena, Marti, Martita,
  Mattie, Matty, Moireach

Martina (Latin) after Mars, the god
  of war
  Feminine form of Martin
  Also Martine, Tina

Mary (Hebrew) bitterness
  Also Mair, Maire, Mame, Mamie,
  Manette, Manon, Mara, Marea,
  Marella, Maretta, Marette, Mari,
  Maria, Mariam, Mariamne, Marian,
  Mariana, Marianna, Marianne,
  Marica, Marie, Mariel, Mariet,
  Marietje, Marietta, Mariette,
  Marika, Marilin, Marilla, Marilyn,
  Marion, Marionette, Mariquita,
  Marita, Mariya, Marja, Marla,
  Marya, Maryanne, Marylin,

Marylon, Marylyn, Maryon,
Maryse, Marysia, Masha, Maura,
Maureen, Maurizia, May, Mearr,
Mija, Miriam, Mitzi, Mo, Moira,
Moire, Molly, Moreena, Morena,
Moya, Moyra, Muire, Polly

Marylou *combination* of Mary and
Louise

Mary-Rose *combination* of Mary and
Rose

Matilda (Old German) mighty and
  strong battle-maid
  Also Maitilde, Matelda, Mathilda,
  Mathilde, Matilde, Maud, Maude,
  Tilly

Matsu (Japanese) happy

Maude *see* Matilda

Maureen (Irish) *see* Mary

Mavis (Old French) the song thrush
  Also Mavas

Maxine (French) the greatest
  Feminine form of Maximilian
  Also Maxima, Maxime

May (Latin) of the month of May
  See also Mary

Maya (Sanskrit) art and wisdom

Megan (Welsh) *see* Margaret

Melaine *see* Melanie

Melanie (Greek) dark or black
Also Melaina, Melaine Melania,
Melantha, Melany, Melena,
Melloney, Mellony, Melony

Melba (Old English) from the mill
stream
Feminine form of Melbourne

Melina *see* Carmel and Melinda

Melinda (Greek) mild and gentle
Also Malinda, Malinde, Melina,
Melynda
See also Linda

Melissa (Greek) honey or honey-bee
Feminine form of Melitus
Also Elita, Malita, Melessa, Melice,
Melisma, Melisse, Melita, Melitta,
Melleta, Mellie, Mellita, Milice,
Millissa, Missi

Melody (Greek) a song

Mercy (Latin) compassion
Also Mena, Mercedes

Meredith (Celtic) protector of the sea

Merryn (English) wave of the sea
Also Merewenna, Meruvina,
Merwin, Morwenna

Meryl (Latin) *see* Muriel

Meta (Latin) ambition or goal

Mia (Italian/Spanish) my own

Michelle (French) one who is like
God
Feminine form of Michael
Also Micaela, Mical, Micala,
Michaela, Michaele, Michaelina,
Michaella, Michel, Michela,
Michele, Michelina, Micheline,
Michellia, Miguela, Miguelita,
Mikaela, Mikala, Miquela

Mignon (French) delicate, dainty
Also Mignonette, Mignonne, Mignot

Mila (Italian) lovable
Also Milo

Mildred (Old English) mild power
Also Mildrid

Millicent (Old German) strong or
energetic worker
Also Melesina, Melicent, Melisande,
Mellicent, Melusine, Milicent,
Milisent, Millisent

Mimi *see* Minette

Minerva (Latin) name of the Roman goddess of wisdom

Minette (Old German) resolute antagonist
Also Mimi

Minna (Old German) loving memory

Mirabel (Latin) admired for her beauty
Also Marabel, Mirabella, Mirabelle, Mirella

Miranda (Latin) worthy to be admired

Miriam *see* Mary
Also Miriamme

Mitzi *see* Mary

Moira (Irish) *see* Mary

Molly (Irish) *see* Mary

Mona (Irish) noble
Also Moyna

Monica (Latin) adviser
Also Monicia, Monika, Monike, Monique

Monique (French) *see* Monica

Morag *see* Sarah

Morgan (Welsh) from the sea
Also Morgaine, Morgana

Morna (Gaelic) beloved
Also Myrna

Morwenna *see* Merryn

Moto (Japanese) source

Muriel (Greek) myrrh, perfume
Also Merl, Merle, Merlina, Merline, Merola, Merrill, Merrilla, Meryl, Muirgheal, Murial, Murieall, Murielle, Myrlene

Musetta (Old French) quiet pastoral song

Myfanwy (Welsh) my fine one
Also Miffany, Myvanwy

Myra (Greek) she who weeps or laments
Also Mira

Myrtle (Greek) plant name
Also Myrtilla

N

Nadia (Russian) hope
  Also Nada, Nadine, Natejda

Nadine *see* Nadia

Nami (Japanese) wave

Nancy *see* Anne

Nannette (French) *see* Anne
  (Hannah)

Naomi (Hebrew) pleasant one
  Also Naoma, Noami, Nomi

Nara (Old Norse) nearest to

Narelle *see* Helen
  Also Norelle

Nastasya (Russian) *see* Anastasia

Nata (Sanskrit) dancer

Natalie (Latin) natal or birth day
  Also Natala, Natale, Natalia,
  Nataline, Natalka, Natasha,
  Nathalia, Nathalie, Natica, Natika
  See also Noeline

Natasha (Russian) *see* Natalie

Natsu (Japanese) summer

Nefertiti (Egyptian) the beautiful one
  has come

Nelda (Old English) elder tree

Nella *see* Helen

Neoma (Greek) the new moon
  Also Neomah

Nerida (Aboriginal) a flower;
  blossom

Nerilee *see* Nerolie

Nerine (Latin) of the sea
  Feminine form of Nereus
  Also Nerice, Nerissa, Nerita

Nerolie (Italian) the black
  Feminine form of Nero
  Also Nerilee

Nesta (Welsh) *see* Agnes

Netta (Latin) pure and neat
  See also Antonia (Antoinette),
  Henrietta, Jane (Jeanette)

Neysa *see* Agnes

Ngaio (Maori) a tree

Ngaire (Maori) flax
  Also Nyree

Ngoc Lan (Vietnamese) a magnolia

Nicole (Greek) the people's victory
  Feminine form of Nicholas
  Also Nichola, Nicola, Nicoletta,
  Nicolette, Nicolina, Nicoline

Nidra (Sanskrit) sleep

Nina (Russian) *see* Anne (Annina)

Nissa (Scandinavian) friendly elf;
  fairy who can only be seen by
  lovers

Noeline (Old German) Christmas
  Feminine form of Noel
  Also Noelie, Noelita, Noella, Noelle

Noelle (French) *see* Noeline

Nola (Celtic) the noble

Nona (Latin) the ninth child
  Also Nonie

Nora (Irish) *see* Helen (Eleanor),
  Honora

Norma (Latin) the norm, rule or
  pattern

Nyree (English) *see* Ngaire

O

Obelia (Greek) related to obelisk (pillar)

Octavia (Latin) the eighth child
Feminine form of Octavius
Also Octavie, Oktavija, Ottavia, Tavia

Odessa (Greek) of the Odyssey

Odette (French) home lover
Also Odala, Odelia, Odella, Odila, Odilla, Odille, Othilia, Otila, Ottilia

Olga (Old German) *see* Helga

Olivia (Latin) the olive tree, symbol of peace
Feminine form of Oliver
Also Olive, Olivette, Olva

Olwen (Welsh) white footprint, clover
Also Olwyn

Olympia (Greek) of Olympus, the home of the gods
Also Olimpia, Olimpias, Olympe, Olympias, Olympie, Pia

Ona/Oona (Lithuanian) *see* Una

Ondine (Latin) *see* Undine

Oneida (North American Indian) the awaited or expected

Opal (Sanskrit) precious stone, jewel

Ophelia (Greek) a serpent; invincible and wise
Also Ofelia, Ofeliga, Ofilia, Ophelie, Phelia

Ora *see* Aurora

Oralia *see* Oriel

Oriana (Latin) the dawning
Also Oriande, Oriante

Oriel (English) a window
Also Oralia

Orlanda (Italian) *see* Rolanda

Orsa/Orsola *see* Ursula

P

Pagan (Latin) villager

Page (English) attendant
Also Paige

Paloma (Spanish) the dove

Pamela (Greek) sweetness
Also Pamelina, Pamella, Pamsin

Pandora (Greek) gifted

Pansofia (Greek) all wisdom
See also Sophia

Pansy (Greek) fragrant flower

Panya (African) a twin child

Paola *see* Paula

Pascha (Middle English) Easter child
Also Paschale, Pasquette

Patience (Latin) endurance

Patricia (Latin) noble, well-born.
Feminine form of Patrick
Also Patreeza, Patrice, Patrizia, Patsy

Paula (Latin) small
Feminine form of Paul
Also Paola, Paolina, Paule, Paulette,
Paulina, Pauline, Paulita, Pavia,
Pavla, Pavlica

Pauline *see* Paula

Pavla (Czechoslovakian) *see* Paula

Pazanne (French) country woman
Also Pezaine

Pearl (Latin) a jewel
Also Pearla, Perle

Peg *see* Margaret

Penelope (Greek) symbol of wifely
fidelity
Also Pennie, Penny

Perdita (Latin) lost

Perizada (Persian) fairy-born

Persis (Greek) Persian woman

Peta *see* Petra

Petra (Greek) stone or rock
Feminine form of Peter
Also Parnel, Peita, Perinna,
Peronella, Perrine, Peta, Petrea,
Petrina, Petriona, Petronella,
Petronia, Petronilla, Petronille,
Pier, Pierella, Pierette, Pierina

Petula (Latin) seeker

Petunia (Indian) a flower

Phaedora (Greek) a gift of God

Phanessa *see* Vanessa

Phedra (Greek) bright
Also Phaedra

Philadelphia (Greek) brotherly love

Philippa (Greek) lover of horses
Feminine form of Philip
Also Felipa, Filippa, Phillipa

Phillida *see* Phyllis

Philomena (Greek) nightingale who
sings to the moon

Phoebe (Greek) goddess of the moon
Also Phebe

Phryne [Frine-ee] (Greek) pale and
delicate

Phyllis (Greek) leafy green bough
Also Fillis, Phillida, Phillyda,
Phyllida, Phyllys

Pia (Latin) devout
See also Olympia

Pier *see* Petra

Placida (Latin) calm

Polly *see* Mary

Poppy (Latin) flower symbolising
peace

Portia (Latin) a harbour, safety

Primrose (Latin) the first rose
See also Rose

Priscilla (Latin) the primitive or
ancient
Also Cilla, Prisca, Priscella

Prudence (Latin) discretion
Also Prudencia, Prudentia

Prunella (French) sloe plum or
prunus

Q

Queenie (English) a pet name for girls called Victoria during the time of that queen's reign
Also Queena, Queeny

Querida (Spanish) beloved

Quintina (Latin) the fifth child
Also Quinta, Quintella, Quintilla

R

Rachel (Hebrew) ewe, symbolising innocence
Also Rachael, Rachela, Rachele, Rachelle, Raechael, Rahel, Raoghnailt, Raquel, Raychela, Shelley

Rae (Scandinavian) a doe

Raina *see* Regina

Ramona (Old German) wise and mighty protector
Feminine form of Raymond
Also Raimonda, Ramonda

Rani (Sanskrit) a royal princess

Raquel *see* Rachel

Rati (Sanskrit) love and desire

Rebecca (Hebrew) compliant wife
Also Rebeca, Rebeccah, Rebeka, Rebekah, Rebekka, Rivkah

Regan *see* Regina

Regina (Latin) queen
Also Raina, Regan, Reina, Reyna

Rei (Japanese) ceremonious

Ren (Japanese) intelligence

Renata (Latin) born again
Also Rena, Renate, Rene, Renee

Renee (French) *see* Renata

Rhea (Greek) poppy; flowering from the earth
Also Rea

Rhian (Welsh) maiden

Rhiannon (Welsh) nymph

Rhoda (Greek) rose
Also Rhodeia, Rhodia

Rhonda (Welsh) after a valley in southern Wales

Rhonwen (Celtic) white skirt

Ria (Spanish) the river
See also Mary (Maria)

Rina (Greek) pure

Riona (Irish) queenly

Rita (Sanskrit) order or law
See also Margaret (Margherita)

Roberta (Old German) bright
shining fame
Feminine form of Robert
Also Bobbette, Robena, Robertina,
Robin, Robina, Robine, Robinetta,
Robinette, Robinia, Robyn, Ruperta

Robyn (Old English) see Roberta

Rochelle (Latin) little rock
Feminine form of Roche
Also Rochella, Rochette

Roesia (Old French) see Rose

Rohana (Sanskrit) sandalwood tree

Rolanda (Old German) fame of the
land
Feminine form of Roland
Also Orlanda

Romola (Latin) fame
Feminine form of Romulo

Rosa see Rose

Rosalie see Rose

Rosalind (Old German) see Rose

Rosamund (Old German) pure or
clean rose
Also Rosamond, Rosamonda,
Rosamunda, Rozamond

Rose (Latin) flower name
Also Ralia, Rasche, Roesia,
Rohesia, Rosa, Rosabel, Rosabella,
Rosalba, Rosaleen, Rosalia,
Rosalie, Rosalija, Rosalind,
Rosalinda, Rosalinde, Roseanna,
Roseanne, Rosel, Roseta, Rosetta,
Rosie, Rosina, Rosita, Roslyn,
Royce, Royse, Roysia, Rozalind,
Rozelle
See also Primrose, Rosemary

Rosemary (Latin) name for herb of
remembrance
Also Rose Marie, Rosemare,
Rosemari, Rosemarie
See also Rose

Rosetta (French) see Rose

Rosina (Italian) see Rose

Rosita (Spanish) see Rose

Rowena (Celtic) white-maned
Also Renwien, Rhonwen

Roxanna (Persian) brilliant
Also Roschana, Roxana, Roxanne,
Roxine

Ruby (English) precious stone

Ruth (Hebrew) kind friend
Also Rutha, Ruthe, Ruthi, Ruthia,
Ruthie

S

Sabah (Arabic) morning

Sabina (Italian) woman of Sabine people in ancient Italy
Also Sabin, Sabine, Sabiny, Saidhghin, Savina

Sabrina (Latin) princess

Sacha (Russian) *see* Alexandra

Sachiko (Japanese) joy

Sadie *see* Sarah

Sai (Japanese) intelligence

Salena (Greek) salty
Also Salina

Sally *see* Sarah

Salome (Hebrew) peaceful

Samantha (Aramaic) listener

Sanchia (Spanish) holy
Also Sancha, Sancta, Sancya

Sandra *see* Alexandra (Alessandra), Cassandra

Sapphire (Hebrew) like a sapphire stone, jewel

Sarah (Hebrew) princess
Also Morag, Sade, Sadella, Sadie, Sadye, Saida, Salaidh, Sallie, Sally, Sara, Saraid, Sarene, Saretta, Sarette, Sari, Sarie, Sarine, Sarita, Sarka, Sayda, Sirri, Sorcha, Zaddah, Zahra, Zara, Zarah, Zaras, Zaria

Sarasa (Sanskrit) beautiful, gracious

Scarlett (Old English) a rich red colour

Selena (Greek) name of the moon goddess
Also Celene, Celie, Celina, Celinda, Celine, Selene, Selina, Selinda

Septima (Latin) seventh child

Seraphina (Hebrew) the enthusiastic believer
Feminine form of Seraph

Also Serafina, Serafine, Seraphia,
Seraphine, Seraphita

Serena (Latin) calm, tranquil

Shaina (Yiddish) beautiful

Shane *see* Jane

Shani (African) wonderful

Shannon (Celtic) slow waters

Shantelle *see* Chantal

Sharleen *see* Caroline

Sharon (Hebrew) a princess
Also Sharee, Sharne, Sharolyn

Shauna (Irish) *see* Jane

Sheba *see* Bathsheba

Sheena (English) *see* Jane (Sine)
Also Sheenah, Shena

Sheila (Irish) *see* Cecilia

Shelley (Old English) from the edge
of the meadow
See also Rachel

Sheryl *see* Cheryl

Shimona (Hebrew) little princess
Also Mona

Shirley (Old English) the shining
meadow
Also Shirlea, Shirlee, Shirleen,
Shirlene, Shirlie

Shona (Celtic) *see* Jane

Sibil *see* Sybil

Sidra (Latin) of the stars

Sigrid (Old Norse) victory ride

Silvana *see* Sylvia
Also Silvaine

Simone (Hebrew) one who hears
Feminine form of Simon
Also Simona, Simonetta, Simonette,
Simonne

Sine (Scottish) *see* Jane

Sinead [Shin-aid] (Irish) *see* Jane

Siobhan [Shoo-vawn] (Irish) *see*
Jane (Joanna)

Sirena (Greek) sweet singer or siren

Sisi (African) born on Sunday

Sita (Sanskrit) furrow

Sofia *see* Sophia

Sondra *see* Alexandra

Sonia (Russian) *see* Sophia

Sophia (Greek) wisdom
Also Beathag, Sadhbh, Sadhbha, Senya, Sifia, Sofia, Sofie, Sonia, Sonja, Sonya, Sophie, Sophy, Zosia, Zsofia

Sorcha (Celtic) *see* Sarah

Stacie *see* Anastasia, Eustacia

Stella (Latin) *see* Esther

Stephanie (French) crown or garland
Feminine form of Stephen
Also Estaphania, Ettienette, Stefanie, Steffanie, Steffie, Stepania, Stephana, Stephania, Stephena, Stevana, Stevania, Stevena, Stevie

Sukie *see* Susan

Susan (Hebrew) lily
Also Sosanna, Su, Sue, Suisan, Suke, Sukey, Sukie, Susana, Susanna, Susannah, Suse, Susette, Susie, Suska, Susy, Suzann, Suzanna, Suzanne, Suze, Suzette, Suzie, Zosa, Zsa Zsa, Zsuzsa, Zusanne

Swanhilda (Old German) swan battle-maiden

Sybil (Greek) prophetess
Also Sevilla, Sibeal, Sibella, Sibelle, Sibil, Sibila, Sibilla, Sibyl, Sibylla, Sibylle, Sybilla, Sybillina, Sybylla

Sydney (Old English) from St Denis
Feminine form of Sidney
Also Cydney Sydnee

Sylvia (Latin) one who lives in the forest
Also Ailvia, Silva, Silvana, Silvia, Silvie, Silvija, Sylva, Sylvana, Zilvia

T

Tabitha (Aramaic) gazelle

Tace (Latin) silence and peace
   Also Tacye

Tacita (Latin) silent

Tahira (Arabic) pure

Tamara (Hebrew) a palm tree
   Also Tamar, Tammie, Tammy

Tammy *see* Tamara

Tamsin *see* Thomasina

Tansy (Latin) tenacious, name for
   the yellow-flowered herb

Tanya *see* Titania

Tara (Gaelic) crag or tower, place
   name of the historic seat of ancient
   Irish kings

Tarra (Aboriginal) creek

Tarn (Scandinavian) mountain lake

Tatiana (Latin) silver-haired
   Also Tatianas, Tatianna, Tatjana

Tatum (Old English) cheerful or
   joyful one
   Feminine form of Tate

Tavia *see* Octavia

Tegan (Celtic) doe

Tempe (Greek) beautiful, delightful,
   charming

Teresa *see* Theresa

Tessa (Greek) *see* Theresa

Thalia (Greek) blooming
   Also Talia

Thanh (Chinese) blue

Thank (Vietnamese) tranquil

Thea (Greek) goddess
   See also Althea, Anthea, Dorothy
   (Dorothea), Theodora

Thecla (Greek) divine
  Also Thecle

Thelma (Greek) nursling
  Also Thelmai

Theodora (Greek) gift of God
  Also Fedora, Feodora, Teodora,
  Thea, Theodosia
  See also Dorothy

Theophila (Greek) loved by God
  Also Theofilia

Theresa (Latin) to harvest
  Also Teresa, Terese, Teresija,
  Teresina, Teresita, Tereza, Terry,
  Tessa, Therese, Theresia, Tracie,
  Tracy, Tresa, Tresca, Tressa

Thetis (Greek) silver-footed

Thomasina (Aramaic) a twin
  Feminine form of Thomas
  Also Tamasine, Tamsin, Tamzin,
  Thomasin, Thomasine

Thora (Old Norse) the thunderer
  Feminine of Thor

Thyrza (Greek) staff or wand

Tiffany (Greek) when God was made
  known

  Also Epifania, Epiphanie,
  Theophania, Tifaine, Tifanie,
  Tiffanie, Tiffeny, Tiphanie

Tina *see* Augusta (Augustina),
  Christine, Clementine, Elizabeth
  (Bettina), Martina, Valentina

Ting (Chinese) graceful

Titania (Greek) titaness
  Also Tania, Tanya

Toinette *see* Antonia (Antoinette)

Tomi (Japanese) rich

Toni *see* Antonia

Tonya (Russian) *see* Antonia

Topaz (Greek) jewel name for a
  precious yellow stone

Tourmaline (Sri Lankan) jewel

Tracy (Old English) bold,
  courageous one
  Also Tracey, Tracie
  See also Theresa

Trixie *see* Beatrice

Trudy (Old German) loved one
See also Gertrude

Tsing (Chinese) pure and subtle

Tuesday (Old English) born on
Tuesday
Also Mardi

Tuyet (Chinese) white as snow

U

Ula (Celtic) jewel of the sea

Ultima (Latin) the ultimate or last

Umeko (Japanese) plum, blossom

Una (Latin) one
 Also Ona, Oona, Oonagh

Undine (Latin) water sprite
 Also Ondine, Undene, Undina

Urania (Greek) the sky

Ursula (Latin) she-bear
 Also Orsa, Orsola, Sula, Ursa, Ursel,
 Ursola, Ursule, Ursulette, Ursulina,
 Ursuline

V

Valda (Old German) a warrior
  Also Valina, Velda

Valentina (Latin) valiant and strong
  one
  Feminine form of Valentine
  Also Valencia, Valentia, Valida

Valerie (Latin) strong and healthy
  one
  Feminine form of Valerian
  Also Valaree, Valeria, Valery,
  Valoree

Valma (Welsh) a mayflower
  Also Valmai

Vanessa (Greek) butterfly
  Also Phanessa, Vanesa

Vanka (Russian) *see* Anne

Vanora (Scottish) *see* Genevieve

Vashti (Persian) beautiful
  Also Vashta, Vashtee, Vashtia

Velda (Old German) inspired wisdom

Velma *see* Wilhelmina

Velvet (Latin) a fleece

Venetia (Latin) *see* Gwyneth

Venus (Latin) the goddess of love

Vera (Latin) faith, truth
  Also Vere, Verena, Verene,
  Veridiana, Verina, Verine, Verity,
  Verla
  See also Veronica

Veridiana (Spanish) *see* Vera

Verity *see* Vera

Veronica (Latin) of or belonging to
  an image
  Also Veronice, Veronike, Veronique
  See also Vera

Victoria (Latin) victorious conquerer
  Feminine form of Victor
  Also Victoire, Victorija, Victorine,
  Viktoria, Vitoria, Vittoria
  See also Queenie

Vida (Hebrew) *see* Davina

Viola (Latin) *see* Violet

Violet (Old French) flower name
Also Ianthe, Iolanda, Iolanthe,
Jolanda, Jolande, Joletta, Viola,
Violante, Viole, Violetta, Violette,
Yolanda, Yolande, Yolante,
Yolanthe, Yolette

Virgilia (Latin) a genus of trees

Virginia (Latin) pure, virgin
Also Virginie

Vita *see* Davina

Vivien (Latin) vital; alive
Feminine form of Vivian
Also Vivian, Viviana, Vivianne,
Vivienne, Vivyan, Vyvian, Vyvyan

W

Wanda (Old German) the wanderer
Also Wandis, Wenda, Wendelin,
Wendeline, Wendy

Wendy *see* Wanda

Wenonah (North American Indian)
first born
Also Wenona, Winona

Wilhelmina (Old German) resolute
protector
Feminine form of William
(Wilhelm)
Also Guglielma, Guillelmina,
Guillelmine, Guillemette, Minella,
Velma, Vilhelmina, Vilma,
Wilhelma, Wilhelmine, Willa,
Willamina, Willette, Wilma,
Wilmette, Wylma

Willow (English) name of a tree

Winifred (Old German) peaceful
friend
Also Winifrid, Winny

Winsome (English) pleasant or
attractive

Wynne (Celtic) fair

Wyterica (Aboriginal) wattle

X Y Z

Xanthe (Greek) golden-haired

Xaviera (Arabic) the saviour

Xenia (Greek) hospitable
  Also Xena, Xene, Zenia

Xylia (Greek) of the forest

Yasmine (Arabic) *see* Jasmine

Yedda (Old German) the singer

Yei (Japanese) flourishing

Yen (Chinese) beautiful, charming, pretty

Yet-Kwai (Chinese) beautiful as a rose

Yetta (Old English) the given

Yoko (Japanese) determined woman

Yolande (Old French) *see* Violet

Yoorana (Aboriginal) loving

Yoshi (Japanese) respectful

Yuri (Japanese) lily

Yvonne (French) the archer
  Feminine form of Yves
  Also Evonne, Ivette, Yevette, Yvette

Zada (Arabic) prosperous
  Also Zadah

Zandra *see* Alexandra

Zane *see* Jane

Zara (Persian) *see* Sarah

Zenda (Persian) womanly
  Also Zendah

Zenobia (Greek) father's ornament
  Also Zenobie, Zenovia

Zerlinda (Hebrew) of the dawn
  Also Zerlina

Zoe (Greek) life
  Also Zoia

Zsa Zsa (Hungarian) *see* Susan

BOYS'
NAMES

A

Aaron (Hebrew) high mountain
Also Aharoun, Aron, Haroun

Abadi (Arabic) eternal

Abbot (Old English) abbey father

Abdul (Arabic) servant, son
Also Abdel

Abdullah (Arabic) servant of Allah

Abel (Hebrew) the breath
Also Abell, Abelot, Able, Hebel

Abner (Hebrew) father of light

Abraham (Hebrew) father of
multitudes
Also Abira, Abrahamo, Abramo,
Arum, Ibrahim

Absalom (Hebrew) father of peace

Abu (Arabic) father
Also Abou

Ace (Hebrew) unity or the unit, one
who excels

Achilles (Greek) without lips
Also Achille

Adair (Scottish) from the oak-tree
ford

Adam (Hebrew) of the red earth
Also Adamo, Adan, Adao, Adhamh

Adrian (Latin) of the Adriatic
Also Adriano, Adrien, Arne, Arrian,
Hadrian

Aeneas *see* Angus

Ahmed [Aak-med] (Arabic) highly
praised

Aidan (Celtic) little fiery one
Also Edan, Egan

Aiken (Old English) the oaken

Ainsley (Old English) Ain's meadow
Also Ainslee, Ainslie

Airlie *see* Earl

Ajax (Greek) earthy

Akira (Japanese) intelligent

Akiyama (Japanese) autumn

Aladdin (Arabic) servant of Allah

Alan (Celtic) handsome, harmonious one
Also Ailean, Ailin, Alain, Aland, Alano, Alawn, Allan, Allen, Allyn, Aluon, Alun, Alunn, Eilian

Alard (Old German) hard and noble

Alaric (Old German) to rule all

Alastair (Gaelic) *see* Alexander

Alban (Latin) white; of Alba
Also Alben, Albin
See also Aubin

Albert (Old German) noble and bright
Also Adalbert, Adelbert, Adelberto, Adelbrecht, Ailbert, Albertino, Alberto, Albrecht, Albret, Aubert, Elbert, Ethelbert

Aldo (Old German) *see* Aldous

Aldous (Old German) from the old house
Also Aldis, Aldo, Aldus

Alexander (Greek) protector of mankind
Also Alasdair, Alastair, Alec, Aleck, Alejandro, Aleksandras, Aleksandre, Aleksandus, Alessandro, Alex, Alexandre, Alexandros, Alexandru, Alexio, Alexis, Alick, Alistair, Alister, Allesandro, Allister, Alsandair, Alysander, Sasha, Xan

Alfred (Old German) elf counsel
Also Alfredo, Alfrid, Alvere, Auvere, Avery

Algernon (French) with the whiskers

Ali (Arabic) exalted one

Alistair (Gaelic) *see* Alexander

Allan/Allen *see* Alan

Allunga (Aboriginal) sun

Almeric (Old German) work to rule
Also Americ, Emeric
See also Eric

Aloysius [Alo-wish-us] (French) *see* Lewis

Alphonso (Old German) noble and ready for battle
Also Affonso, Alfons, Alfonse, Alonso, Alonzo, Alphonso, Alphonsus

Alton (Old English) dweller in the old town

Alvin (Old German) friend of all or noble friend
Also Aloin, Alvan, Alvino, Alwin, Alwyn, Elvin

Alvis *see* Elvis

Amadeus (Latin) beloved of God

Ambrose (Greek) immortal one
Also Ambrogio, Ambroise, Ambros, Ambrosi, Ambrosio, Ambrosius, Ambroz, Ambrozij

Amery (Old French) divine
Also Amory, Emery

Amos (Hebrew) strong, courageous

Ananda (Sanskrit) a blessing

Anders (Scandinavian) *see* Andrew

Andre (French) *see* Andrew

Andrew (Greek) strong or manly
Also Aindreas, Anders, Andre, Andreadis, Andreas, Andrei, Andreiu, Andres, Andrey, Andrzej

Angel (Greek) a heavenly messenger
Also Agnolo, Angelo

Angus (Scottish) unique choice
Also Aeneas, Aonghus

Anka (Aboriginal) barramundi

Anoki (North American Indian) actor

Anthony (Latin) inestimable; beyond price
Also Anntoin, Anthin, Anti, Antoine, Anton, Antonij, Antonin, Antonio, Antonius, Antony, Tonio, Tony

Apollo (Greek) name of the sun god

Aquila (Latin) eagle

Archibald (German) noble and truly bold
Also Achimbald, Archaimbauld, Archambault, Arcibaldo, Gilleasbuig

Arden (Old English) dwelling place

Arian (Greek) of Aries, the god of war
  Also Arianus, Arius

Ariel (Hebrew) lion of God

Aristotle (Greek) best of the thinkers

Armand (French) *see* Herman

Armstrong (Old English) strong arm

Arnold (Old German) powerful eagle
  Also Arend, Arnaldo, Arnaud, Arne,
  Arnhold, Arno, Arnoldo, Arnoud,
  Arnulfo, Arny

Arthur (Celtic) strong as a bear
  Also Artair, Artor, Artur, Arturo,
  Artus

Asa (Hebrew) healer

Asbjorn (Norse) divine bear

Ascott (Old English) eastern cottage

Asher (Hebrew) happy one or
  laughing one

Ashley (Old English) of the ash tree
  Also Ashford, Ashlee

Aston (Old English) eastern place

Atalik (Hungarian) like his father

Athol (Scottish) place name
  Also Athole

Aubin (Old French) blond
  Also Aubin, Auburn, Aubyn
  See also Alban

Aubrey (Old French) king of the
  fairies
  Also Auberon, Oberon

Augustine (Latin) venerated
  Also Agostino, Agoston, Auguistin,
  Austen, Austin
  See also Augustus

Augustus (Latin) the high, honoured,
  mighty
  Also Agosto, August, Auguste,
  Augusto
  See also Augustine

Austin *see* Augustine

Avery (Old English) *see* Alfred

Axel (Old Norse) divine peace

Aylmer (Old English) noble and
  famous
  Also Elmer

B

Baden (German) bath

Bailey (Old French) bailiff
Also Baily

Baldric (Old German) bold ruler

Baldwin (Old German) bold
protector
Also Baldovino, Baudoin, Baudouin,
Boden, Bowden, Maldwyn

Banquo (Celtic) white
Also Banan

Baptist (Greek) one who baptises
Also Baptiste, Battiste

Bard (Irish-Gaelic) poet and singer

Barnaby (Aramaic) son of
consolation
Also Barna, Barnaba, Barnabas,
Barnabe, Barnabus, Barnebas,
Barney, Bernabe

Barnard *see* Bernard

Barret (Old German) bear rule
Also Barrett

Barry (Celtic) fine marksman, spear
Also Barrie

Bartholomew (Hebrew) son of
Talmai, war-like son
Also Bart, Bartek, Bartel,
Bartelemy, Barthel, Barthelemi,
Bartholomaus, Bartholome,
Bartolomeo, Bartolomeus, Barton,
Parlan

Basil (Greek) kingly, royal
Also Basile, Basileos, Basilio,
Basilius, Bazel, Vasilos, Vassily

Bastian *see* Sebastian

Baxter (Old English) baker

Beau (French) handsome

Beaumont (Old French) the beautiful
mountain

Beauregard (Old French) handsome
face

Bede (Old German) prayer

Ben (Hebrew) son
Also Benn
See also Benedict, Benjamin, Benoni

Benedict (Latin) the blessed and of the benediction
Also Bendix, Benedetto, Benedick, Benedicto, Benedictus, Benedikt, Benedix, Bengt, Benito, Bennett, Benoit, Benzel

Benjamin (Hebrew) son of my right hand
Also Bannerjee, Beathan, Beniamino
See also Benson

Bennett (English) *see* Benedict

Benson (Hebrew-English) son of Benjamin

Benvenuto (Italian) the right way

Berenger (Old German) a bear, spear

Bernard (Old German) as brave as a bear
Also Barnard, Barnett, Bearnard, Bernardo, Bernat, Berngard, Bernhard, Bernhart, Burnard

Berthold (Old German) bright ruler
Also Berthoud, Bertolde, Bertoldi, Bertolt, Bertuccio

Bertram (Old German) bright raven
Also Bartok, Bartram, Beltran, Bertrand, Bertrando

Bevan (Celtic) a young archer
Also Beavan, Beaven, Beven, Bevin

Biloela (Aboriginal) cockatoo

Bjorn (Scandinavian) bear

Blaine (Old English) to bubble or blow
Also Blain, Blane, Blayne

Blair (Celtic) a place, a suitable battle-field

Blaise (Latin) stammerer
Also Biagio, Blas, Blase, Blasien, Blasio, Blasius, Blayse, Blaze

Blake (Old English) dark or black

Bland (Latin) mild and gentle

Bob *see* Robert

Bonar (Old French) courteous

Boris (Russian) a fighter

Bowen (Celtic) son of Owen

Boyce (French) of the woods

Boyd (Celtic) fair-haired

Braden (Old English) from the broad valley

Bradford (Old English) from the broad river crossing

Bradley (Old English) from the broad meadow
Also Brad, Bradlee

Brand (Old English) firebrand

Brandon (Celtic) raven
Also Brandan, Branwell

Bray (Old English) brow of the hill

Brecon (Welsh) after the mountains in Wales, the Brecon Beacons

Breese (Old English) son of Rhees

Brendan (Celtic) dweller by the beacon
Also Bredon

Brenton (Old English) the steep or the tall and erect
Also Brent

Brett (Celtic) from Brittany or a Breton

Brewster (Old German) a brewer

Brian (Celtic) strength
Also Branko, Briano, Briant, Brien, Brion, Bryan, Bryant, Bryon

Brice (Celtic) swift or ambitious
Also Bricot, Brisson, Bryce, Bryson

Brinsley (Old English) Brin's meadow
Also Brinsleigh

Brock (Old English) a badger

Broderick (Middle English) from the broad ridge

Brodie (Irish) a ditch
Also Brody

Bruce (Old French) of the brush or of the thicket

Bruno (German) brown

Burleigh (Old English) fort in a clearing
Also Burl, Burley, Burly
See also Burton

Burton (Old English) dweller at the fortified town

Bryan *see* Brian

Bryce *see* Brice

Byron (Middle English) from the cottage or cowman

C

Caalang (Aboriginal) sassafras

Cadman (Celtic) warrior

Cadmus (Greek) to the east

Caesar (Latin) long head of hair
 Also Casar, Caesario, Caesarius,
 Cesar, Cesare

Caffar (Celtic) helmet

Cain (Hebrew) possessed
 Also Caine

Caleb (Hebrew) bold and impetuous

Callaghan (Irish) strife
 Also Callahan

Callangun (Aboriginal) blue fig

Callum (Gaelic) *see* Columba

Calvin (Latin) the bald

Cameron (Gaelic) crooked nose

Camillus (Etruscan) attendant at
 religious ceremonies
 Also Camille, Camillo

Campbell (Gaelic) curved mouth

Cardo (Aboriginal) man

Carl (German) *see* Charles

Carlos (Spanish) *see* Charles

Carrick (Irish) rocky headland

Carroll (Celtic) champion fighter or
 warrior

Carter (Old English) maker or driver
 of carts

Cary (Celtic) one who lives in a castle
 Also Carey
 See also Charles

Casey (Irish) brave

Casimir (Polish) proclamation of
 peace
 Also Kasimir

Caspar *see* Gaspar

Cassidy (Irish) clever

Cassius (Latin) vain

Cecil (Latin) blind
Also Cecile, Ceilius

Cedric (Old English) bounteous and
friendly

Ceri *see* Kerry

Chad (Old English) warrior

Chaim (Hebrew) life
Also Hyram

Chandler (Old French) candle
maker

Chandra (Sanskrit) moon

Charles (Old German) virile and
strong man
Also Carey, Carl, Carlo, Carlos,
Carolus, Cary, Karel, Karl, Karoly,
Tearlach

Charlton (Old English) of the
Charles' or man's farm
Also Carleton, Carlton

Chauncey (French) chancellor,
church official

Cheng (Chinese) accomplish,
succeed

Chester (Latin) of the fortified camp

Chilton (Old English) of the
children's farm

Christian (Latin) a Christian
Also Chrestien, Chretien, Christen,
Christiano, Christien, Karstin,
Krispin, Kristian, Kruschan

Christopher (Greek) bearer of Christ
Also Christof, Christofer,
Christoforo, Christoph,
Christophe, Christophorus,
Christoval, Cristobal, Crysteffor,
Gillecriosd, Kristof, Kristofor,
Kristopas, Kristopher, Kristova

Chun (Chinese) spring

Clarence (Latin) illustrious or bright
Also Clancy

Clark (Old English) a learned man or
cleric

Claude (Latin) the lame
Also Claud, Claudio, Claudius, Klaud

Claus *see* Nicholas

Clayton (Old English) dweller in the clay town
Also Clay

Clement (Latin) merciful
Also Clemens, Clemente, Clementius, Clemento, Keleman, Klemens

Clifford (Old English) of the cliff ford
Also Cliff

Clinton (Old English) hilltop town
Also Clint

Clive (English) cliff

Clunies (Gaelic) resting place

Cohen (Hebrew) priest

Colby (Old English) of Cole's farm

Cole (Celtic) pledge

Colin *see* Columba

Columba (Latin) dove
Also Cailean, Callum, Colan, Colin, Collin, Colum
See also Malcolm

Conan (Celtic) high and mighty
Also Conal, Connell, Konan, Kynan

Connor (Irish) lofty aims or high desire
Also Conor

Conrad (Old German) wise or bold adviser
Also Conrade, Conrado, Cort, Koenraad, Konrad, Konradin, Kort, Kurt

Conroy (Irish) wise man

Constantine (Latin) firm in faith
Also Constantin, Constantino, Constantinos, Kastaden, Konstantin, Kostodon

Corbin (Old French) raven

Cornelius (Latin) a horn
Also Corneille, Cornelio, Cornelis, Kornelius

Cosmo (Greek) order and harmony
Also Cosimo, Cosme

Courtney (Old French) dweller at court

Craig (Celtic) from the stony hill or crag

Crichton (Gaelic) boundary
  Also Creighton

Crispin (Latin) curly haired
  Also Crispianus, Crispino, Crispo,
  Crispus, Krispijn, Krispin

Curtis (Old French) courteous
  Also Curt, Kurt

Cuthbert (Old English) famous,
  bright

Cyrano (Greek) of Cyrene

Cyriack (Greek) lordly
  Also Syriack

Cyril (Greek) lord and master
  Also Cirillo, Cirilo, Cyrill, Cyrille,
  Cyrillus

Cyrus (Greek) throne

D

Dale (Old English) from the dale or valley

Damian *see* Damon

Damon (Greek) the tamed or taming
  Also Damian, Damiano, Damiao, Damien, Damir

Dane (English) from Denmark
  Also Dana

Daniel (Hebrew) God is my judge
  Also Danelo, Danilo, Dannel, Taniel

Dante (Italian) long-lasting
  Also Duran, Durand

Darcy (Old French) from the ark or stronghold
  Also D'Arcy

Darius (Persian) possessing wealth
  Also Darian, Darien

Darrell (Old English) darling or beloved one
  Also Darrel, Daryl, Derrell

Darren (Gaelic) little one
  Also Daran, Darrin, Dorian

David (Hebrew) beloved; loved by God
  Also Dafod, Daibidh, Davidas, Davidde, Davide, Davis, Dawfydd, Dawud, Devi, Dewi, Taffy, Tavid

Davis *see* David

Dean (Old English) from the valley
  Also Deane, Dene

Decimus (Latin) tenth child

Delano (French) of the night

Demetrios (Greek) sacred
  Also Demetri, Dimitry

Dennis (Greek) follower of the god of wine, Dionysos
  Also Denis, Denys, Dion, Dionigio, Dionisio, Dionysius, Dionysos

Denzil (Cornish) high
  Also Denzell

Deodatus (Latin) given by or to God
Also Deodonatus

Derek (German) ruler of the people
Also Derk, Derrick, Deryk,
Diederich, Dirck, Dirk

Dermot (Celtic) a free man
Also Dermott, Diarmaid, Diarmid,
Diarmit, Duibhne

Derwin (Old English) beloved friend
Also Derryn, Derwyn

Desmond (Irish) man of South
Munster

Dexter (Latin) right-handed or skilful
man

Dillon (Gaelic) faithful one
Also Dylan

Dirk *see* Derek

Dobroslav (Slavonic) glorious

Dominic (Latin) belonging to the Lord
Also Domingo, Dominichino,
Dominick, Dominik, Dominique,
Domnech

Donald (Gaelic) prince of the
universe; ruler of the world
Also Donal, Donley, Donnal,
Donnell, Tauno

Donatien (French) given
Also Donat, Donatus, Donnet

Donovan (Irish) dark brown

Dorian *see* Darren

Dougal *see* Dugald

Douglas (Celtic) from the dark blue
water
Also Douglass

Doyle (Irish) dark foreigner

Dudley (Old English) from the lea or
meadow

Dugald (Irish) dark stranger
Also Dougal

Duncan (Celtic) brown warrior

Durand (French) *see* Dante

Dwayne (Gaelic) little dark one
Also Duane

Dwight (English) white or blond one

Dylan (Welsh) man of the sea
Also Dillon

E

Eamon (Irish) *see* Edmund

Earl (Old English) nobleman or chief
 Also Airlie, Earle, Erle, Errol

Ebenezer (Hebrew) stone of help

Edgar (Old English) bright or lucky spear
 Also Eadgar, Edgard, Edgardo

Edmund (Old English) prosperous protector
 Also Eadmund, Eamon, Edmond, Edmondo, Emmon

Edsel (Old English) rich hall

Edward (Old English) prosperous friend or guardian
 Also Duarte, Edouard, Eduard, Eduardo, Eduart, Edvard, Edwardo, Edwardus

Edwin (Old English) rich or happy friend
 Also Eduino, Edwyn

Egan *see* Aidan

Egbert (Old English) bright sword

Egor (Russian) *see* George

Eldred (Old English) old counsel
 Also Aldred

Eleazar (Hebrew) the Lord is helper

Eli *see* Elias

Elias (Hebrew) Jehovah is God
 Also Eli, Elia, Elijah, Elijas, Elisha, Elliot, Elliott, Ellis, Ely

Ellery (English) sweetly spoken

Elliot (English) *see* Elias

Ellis (English) *see* Elias

Elmer *see* Aylmer

Elroy (Old French) the king

Elton (Old English) of the old town
 Also Alton

Elvis (Old Norse) all wise
 Also Alvis

Emery (Old German) to work and rule
 Also Amerigo, Amery, Emeri,
 Emeric, Emerson, Emmery, Emory

Emil (Old German) industrious
 Also Emile, Emilio

Emmanuel (Hebrew) God is with us
 Also Emanuel, Emanuele, Immanuel
 See also Manuel

Emmett (Old English) meeting
 streams
 Also Emmet, Emmit, Emmott

Enrico (Italian) *see* Henry

Enzio (Italian) *see* Henry

Ephraim (Hebrew) doubly fruitful
 Also Ephram, Ephrem

Erasmus (Greek) desired or friendly

Ercole (Italian) *see* Hercules

Erhard (Old German) strong and
 resolved

Eric (Old Norse) powerful ruler
 Also Eirik, Erich, Erick, Erih, Erik,
 Errki

Ernest (Old German) earnest
 Also Eernest, Ernesto, Ernestus,
 Ernst, Hernais

Errol *see* Earl

Erwin *see* Irving

Esau (Hebrew) hairy

Esmond (Old English) grace, beauty

Ethan (Hebrew) steadfast, strong

Ethelbert *see* Albert

Etienne (French) *see* Stephen

Euan *see* Evan

Eubule (Greek) he of good counsel

Eudo (Old Norse) child

Eugene (Greek) nobility, excellence
 Also Eugen, Eugenij, Eugenio,
 Eugenius, Yevgenij

Eustace (Greek) fruitful
 Also Eustachas, Eustache,
 Eustachio, Eustaquio, Eustas

Evan (Welsh) the young
  Also Euan, Ewan, Ewen, Jevon,
  Owen
  See also John

Everard (Old English) strong or
  brave as a boar
  Also Eberhard, Eberhart, Everado,
  Evered, Everett, Everhart, Evraud

Ewen *see* Evan

Ezekiel (Hebrew) strength of God
  Also Ezechiel, Ezechiele, Ezequiel

Ezra (Hebrew) helper
  Also Esdras, Esra

F

Fabian (Latin) ancient Roman family name derived from bean grower
Also Fabien, Fabio, Fabius, Fafiano

Fabrice (French) mechanic
Also Fabrician, Fabricius

Fagan (Gaelic) fiery one
Also Fagin

Faramond (Old German) journey, protection

Farley (Old English) clearing with ferns
Also Farleigh

Farouk (Arabic) to know right from wrong

Farquhar (Gaelic) manly, brave

Faustas (Latin) fortunate, lucky
Also Faust, Faustus

Felix (Latin) happy
Also Felice, Feliks, Phelim

Ferdinand (Old German) adventurer

Also Ferdinando, Fernando, Ferrand, Ferrante, Hernando

Fergus (Celtic) the best choice
Also Fearghas, Feargus

Ferris (Irish) *see* Peter

Fidel (Latin) faithful
Also Fidele, Fidelio, Fildes, Filelio

Findlay (Celtic) fair hero
Also Finlay, Finn

Finian (Celtic) fair child

Flannan (Celtic) blood-red

Fletcher (Old French) arrow-maker and seller

Florian (Latin) flourishing

Floyd *see* Lloyd

Flynn (Irish) son of the red-haired one

Forbes (Scottish) man of prosperity, owner of many fields

Francis (Latin) free; a Frenchman
   Also Ferenc, Francesco, Franchot,
   Francisco, Franciskus, Franciszek,
   Franco, Francois, Frane, Frank,
   Frans, Frants, Franz, Franzisk

Frank *see* Francis

Franklin (Middle English) not in
   bondage, freeholder
   Also Francklin, Franklyn

Fraser (Old English) curly-haired
   Also Frazer

Frederick (Old German) peaceful
   ruler
   Also Farruco, Frederic, Frederico,
   Fredericus, Frederigo, Frederik,
   Frederikos, Fredric, Fredrik,
   Freerik, Fridrich, Friedrich, Fritz

Fu (Chinese) man

Fu-Hai (Chinese) man of the lake

G

Gabor (Hungarian) *see* Gabriel

Gabriel (Hebrew) messenger of God
Also Gabel, Gabela, Gabor,
Gabriele, Gabriello, Gavril

Gamel (Old Norse) old

Gandolfo (German) progress of the
wolf

Garcia (Spanish) *see* Gerald

Gareth (Welsh) gentle
See also Gary

Garfield (Old English) field of war
See also Gary

Garnet (Middle English) dark red
stone

Garth (Old Norse) from the garden,
a yardkeeper

Gary *diminutive* of Gareth, Garfield
and Gerald
Also Garey, Gari, Garrie

Gaspar (Persian) treasure master
Also Caspar, Casper, Gaspard,
Gaspardo, Gasparo, Gasper,
Jasper, Kaspar, Kaspe, Kasper

Gaspard (French) *see* Gaspar

Gaston (French) from Gascony

Gavin (Welsh) white hawk
Also Gauvain, Gavan, Gaven,
Gawain, Gawayne, Gawen, Gawin

Gayadari (Aboriginal) platypus

Gene *see* Eugene

Geoffrey (Old German) divine peace
Also Geoff, Geoffroi, Giofredo,
Godfrey, Godofredo, Gofredo,
Gotfryd, Jeffery, Jeffrey, Jeffroi

George (Greek) tiller of the soil
Also Djuro, Egor, Georas, Georg,
Georges, Georgius, Giorgio,
Gyorgy, Igor, Jerzy, Jiri, Jorge,
Seiorse, Yorick, Yrjo, Yuri

Gerald (Old German) spear and rule
Also Garcia, Gearalt, Geralde, Geraud, Gerold, Gerrit, Gerry, Gieraud, Giraldo

Gerard (Old German) spear and hard
Also Garrett, Gebhard, Gerardo, Geraud, Gerhard, Gerhart, Gerry, Gherardino

Gerry *see* Gerald and Gerard

Gervaise (French) *see* Jarvis

Gianninno (Italian) *see* John

Gideon (Hebrew) faller or hewer

Gifford (Old German) bold gift

Gil (Hebrew) joy
See also Gilbert, Giles

Gilbert (Old German) bright pledge
Also Gilbertas, Gilberto, Gilibeirt, Gilleabart, Giselbert, Guilbert

Gilchrist (Gaelic) servant of Christ

Giles (Greek) youthful; wearer of the goatskin
Also Egide, Egidio, Egidius, Gil, Gilles, Gillie

Giorgio (Italian) *see* George

Giovanni (Italian) *see* John

Glen (Celtic) of the glen or valley
Also Glenn, Glyn, Glynn, Glynne

Goddard (Old German) God and hard

Godfrey *see* Geoffrey

Godwin (Old English) God's friend

Goldwin (Old English) golden friend

Gonzales (Spanish) wolf of war
Also Gonzalo

Goonagulla (Aboriginal) sky

Goonaroo (Aboriginal) whistling duck

Gordon (Gaelic) from the cornered hill
Also Gordan, Gorden

Gough (Welsh) red-haired

Graeme *see* Graham

Graham (Old English) from the grey home
Also Graeme, Grahame, Grame

Grant (Old French) the great or tall one

Grantham (Old English) the big meadow
Also Grantland, Grantley

Granville (Old French) from the great estate or town

Gregory (Greek) vigilant or watchful
Also Greagoir, Greg, Gregg, Gregoire, Gregor, Gregorie, Gregorio, Gregorius, Gregos, Greig, Grigg, Grigor, Grigori, Grigorij, Grigory, Griogair, Grioghar

Guilhermo (Spanish) *see* William

Guiseppe (Italian) *see* Joseph

Gunther (German) battle army
Also Gunthar

Gustavus (Old German) staff of God
Also Gustav

Guy (Old French) a guide
Also Guido

H

Habib (Arabic) the beloved

Hacon (Old Norse) useful, handy
Also Haakon

Hadden (Old English) from the
heather of the moors
Also Haden

Hadrian *see* Adrian

Hagan (Gaelic) the young one

Hai (Chinese) of the sea or lake

Hamilton (Scottish) crooked hill

Hamish (Gaelic) *see* Jacob (James)

Hamon (Old German) house or home

Hannibal (Phoenician) by the grace
of Baal

Hans (German) *see* John

Hardy (Old German) robust and
enduring

Harold (Old English) ruler of the
army
Also Aralt, Harailt, Harald,
Haroldas, Harris, Harry, Herold

Harrimiah (Aboriginal) mythical
black goanna

Harry *see* Harold and Henry

Harvey (Breton) battle-worthy
Also Hervey

Hayden (Old English) from the
hedge or valley
Also Haydon, Haydn

Heath (Old English) from the heath
or heather

Heathcliff (Old English) cliff and
heather

Heathcote (Old English) cottage
among the heath

Hector (Greek) steadfast
Also Ettore

Heinrich (German) *see* Henry

Helmut (German) courage and fame

Henry (Old German) home ruler
Also Eanruig, Enrico, Enrikas,
Enrique, Enzio, Hamlyn, Hanraoi,
Harry, Heikki, Heine, Heinrich,
Heinz, Hendrick, Hendrik, Henk,
Henri, Henrici, Henricus, Henrik,
Henriot, Henrique

Herbert (Old German) brilliant
warrior
Also Eberto, Harbert, Hebert,
Herbertas, Heriberto, Hoireabard

Hercules (Greek) lordly fame
Also Ercole, Heracles, Hercule

Herman (Old German) warrior
Also Armand, Armando, Armant,
Armin, Ermanno, Ermin, Harman,
Harmann, Harmon, Hermando,
Hermon

Hermes (Greek) noble

Hilary (Latin) cheerful and merry
Also Hilaire, Hilario, Hillary, Hillery,
Ilario

Hiram (Hebrew) God is high

Hoa (Vietnamese) peace-loving

Homer (Greek) pledge, security
Also Homere, Homerus, Omero

Horace (Latin) keeper of the hours
of light
Also Horacio, Horatio, Horatius,
Horats, Orazio

Howard (Old English) brave in heart
and mind

Hu (Chinese) a tiger, brave

Hubert (Old German) bright heart
and mind
Also Hoibeard, Huberto, Hugibert,
Ulberto

Hugh (Old German) thoughtful mind
Also Aodh, Aoidh, Hu, Hugo,
Hugues, Ugo

Hugo (German) *see* Hugh

Humphrey (Old German) protector of peace
Also Humfrey, Humfrid, Humfried, Humfry, Hunfredo, Onfroi, Onofre, Onofredo

Hung (Vietnamese) strong, powerful

Hwang Fu (Chinese) rich future

Hyram *see* Chaim

I

Ian (Scottish) *see* John

Ignatius (Latin) ardent; fiery
Also Ignace, Ignacio, Ignatus, Ignaz, Ignazio, Inigo

Igor (Russian) *see* George

Immanuel *see* Emmanuel

Ingemar (Old Norse) famous son
Also Ingmar

Ira (Hebrew) a watcher

Irving (Old English) friend of the sea
Also Erwin, Irvin, Irvine, Irwin

Isaac (Hebrew) laughter
Also Isaak, Isacco, Izaak

Isaiah (Hebrew) God is helper

Isas (Japanese) meritorious

Israel (Hebrew) ruling with the Lord

Ivan (Russian) *see* John

Ives *see* Yves

Ivo *see* Yves

Ivor (Norse) archer
Also Ifor, Ivar, Iver

J

Jabez (Hebrew) height

Jack *see* John

Jackson (Old English) son of Jack

Jacob (Hebrew) supplanter
Also Diego, Giacobbe, Giacobo, Giacomo, Giacopo, Hamish, Iachimo, Iacovo, Iago, Jacabo, Jaco, Jacobus, Jacques, Jaime, Jakab, Jake, Jakob, Jakov, James, Jan, Jascha, Jayme, Jens, Seamus, Shamus

Jacques (French) *see* Jacob

James *see* Jacob

Jan *see* Jacob, John

Janos (Hungarian) *see* John

Jared (Hebrew) to descend
Also Jaret, Jareth, Jarrath, Jarrod

Jarvis (Old German) sharp spear
Also Gervaise, Jervis

Jason (Greek) healer

Jasper *see* Gaspar

Jean (French) *see* John

Jedidiah (Hebrew) God's friend
Also Jed

Jeffrey *see* Geoffrey

Jeremy (Hebrew) exalted by the Lord
Also Diarmaidh, Geremia, Jeremiah, Jeremias

Jerome (Greek) the holy name
Also Gerome, Geronimo, Jeronimus, Jerrome

Jesse (Hebrew) God's grace; he beholds

Jethro (Hebrew) abundance or excellence

Jevon (Welsh) *see* Evan

Jiang (Chinese) river

Jivanta (Sanskrit) long-lived

Joachim (Hebrew) God will
establish
Also Joaquin

Jocelyn *see* Justin

Joel (Hebrew) the Lord is God

Johann (German) *see* John

John (Hebrew) God is gracious
Also Eoghan, Eoin, Evan, Gian,
Gianninno, Giovanni, Hannu, Hans,
Iaian, Iain, Ian, Iannis, Ioan, Ivan,
Jack, Jan, Janos, Jean, Joao, Jock,
Johann, Johannes, Jon, Jones,
Jonn, Jovica, Juan, Jussi, Seain,
Sean, Seann, Shane, Shawn,
Yiannis, Zane

Jonas (Hebrew) the dove
Also Jonah

Jonathan (Hebrew) gift of the Lord
Also Jonathon, Jonothon

Jordan (Hebrew) to descend
Also Gioidana, Jordanes, Jourdain

Joseph (Hebrew) increaser
Also Guiseppe, Josep, Josip, Jossif,
Jozef, Seosaidh, Yusuf

Joshua (Hebrew) God saves

Josiah (Hebrew) healed by the Lord
Also Josias

Juan *see* John

Jude (Hebrew) praise

Jules (French) *see* Julius

Julian *see* Julius

Julius (Latin) youthful one
Also Giulio, Jules, Julian, Juliao,
Julien, Julio, Julion, Julot

Justin (Latin) the just
Also Guistino, Iestin, Jocelin,
Jocelyn, Joslyn, Justino, Justis,
Justus, Justyn

K

Kafir (Arabic) infidel

Kai (Persian) king

Kambara (Aboriginal) crocodile

Kane (Celtic) radiant; bright
  Also Caine, Kayne

Karl (German) *see* Charles

Kaspar *see* Gaspar

Keegan (Irish) little high-spirited
one

Keenan (Irish) little ancient one
  Also Kienan, Kynan

Kieron (Celtic) black

Keith (Gaelic) wood

Kelly (Irish) warrior
  Also Kelley

Kelsey (Old Norse) from the water

Kelvin (Old English) sailor's friend
  Also Kelvan, Kelven

Kelwin (Celtic) dweller by the water

Kendall (Celtic) chief of the valley
  Also Kendal

Kenelm (Old English) brave helmet
  Also Cenhelm

Kenneth (Gaelic) handsome one
  Also Cennydd

Kenrick (Old English) royal ruler

Kent (Welsh) bright one

Kenward (Old English) brave guard

Kerry (Irish) dark one
  Also Ceri

Kevin (Irish) handsome or kind
  Also Kevan, Keven

Kieren (Irish) small and dark
  Also Cairan, Kieran, Kieron, Piran

Kim *see* Kimberley

Kimba (Aboriginal) bush fire

Kimberley (Old English) one who
rules
Also Kim

Kingsley (Old English) of the king's
meadow

Kirk (Old Norse) a place by the
church

Kit *see* Christian and Christopher

Kobi (Aboriginal) medicine man

Koiranah (Aboriginal) eagle

Konrad *see* Conrad

Krishna (Sanskrit) black

Krispin *see* Christian and Crispin

Kuracca (Aboriginal) crestless white
cockatoo

Kurrawa (Aboriginal) rough sea

Kurrin (Aboriginal) sand

Kurt (German) *see* Conrad and
Curtis

Kuyan (Aboriginal) honey bee

Kyena (Aboriginal) barracouta

Kyle (Gaelic) fair and handsome

L

Lachlan (Scottish) war-like
Also Laughlan

Ladislav (Slavonic) glory, power
Also Ladislaus, Laszlo, Laszolo

Lambert (Old German) bright land
Also Lambard, Lamberto

Lamont (Old Norse) law man
Also Lamond

Lance (Old German) land
Also Lancelin, Lancelot, Lanzo,
Launcelot

Lancelot (French) *see* Lance

Lang (Old German) the long or the
tall

Larry *see* Laurence

Lars (Scandinavian) *see* Laurence

Laszlo (Hungarian) *see* Ladislav

Lateef (Arabic) gentle and pleasant

Latimer (Old French) teacher of
Latin

Laurence (Latin) crowned with
laurel
Also Labhras, Labhruinn, Larrance,
Lars, Laurans, Lauren, Laurens,
Laurent, Laurenz, Laurie, Lauritz,
Lawrance, Lawrence, Loren,
Lorenz, Lorenzo, Lourenco

Lazarus (Hebrew) one who God
helps
Also Lazare, Lazaro, Lazzaro, Lazzo

Lee (Old English) a meadow or
clearing
Also Leigh

Leif (Scandinavian) love
Also Leiv, Lief

Leigh *see* Lee

Leith (Celtic) wide

Leo (Latin) the lion
Also Leon, Levin, Lionel, Lionello,
Lyle, Lyonell

Leonard (Old German) as strong as a lion
Also Leanardas, Lennard, Leonardo, Leonerd, Leonhard, Leonid, Lionardo

Leopold (Old German) bold people
Also Leopoldo, Leupold, Luitpold

Leroy (Old French) a king

Leslie (Scottish) from the grey stronghold

Lester (Old English) from Leicester
Also Leicester

Levi (Hebrew) pledge, united

Lewis (Old German) to hear and fight
Also Alois, Aloys, Aloysius, Clovis, Lajos, Lodewijk, Lodovico, Louis, Ludovic, Ludovicus, Ludvig, Ludwig, Lugaidh, Luigi, Luis, Luiz, Luthais

Liam (Irish) *see* William

Lincoln (Celtic) from the colony by the pool

Lindsay (Old English) of the linden tree

Also Linden, Lindley, Lindon, Lindsey, Linsay, Linsey, Lyndon

Linus (Greek) flax-coloured hair

Lionel (Old French) *see* Leo

Llewellyn (Old Welsh) lion-like leader
Also Leoline, Llewllyn

Lloyd (Welsh) the grey
Also Floyd

Lok (Chinese) happiness

Louis (Old French) *see* Lewis

Loy (Chinese) open

Lucian *see* Luke

Ludovic *see* Lewis

Luke (Latin) light
Also Loukas, Luc, Luca, Lucais, Lucas, Lucian, Luciano, Lucien, Lucio, Lucius, Lukas, Lukaz, Luzio

Lyle *see* Leo

Lyndon *see* Lindsay

M

Magnus (Latin) the great
  Also Manus

Malachi (Hebrew) messenger of God
  Also Malachy

Malcolm (Gaelic) servant of St
  Columba

Malise (Gaelic) servant of Jesus

Malory (Old French) luckless
  Also Mallory

Manfred (German) peaceful man

Mani (Aboriginal) equal

Manning (Old English) son of a good
  man

Manuel (Spanish) God with us
  Also Manovello
  See also Emmanuel

Marcel (French) *see* Mark

Mario (Italian) *see* Mark

Mark (Latin) after Mars, the god of
  war
  Also Marc, Marcel, Marcello,
  Marcellus, Marcelo, Marco,
  Marcos, Marcus, Mario, Marius,
  Marko, Markos, Markus
  See also Martin

Marmaduke (Celtic) servant of
  Madoc

Marshall (Old French) the steward

Martin (Latin) after Mars, the god of
  war
  Also Martainn, Marten, Marti,
  Martijn, Martino, Marton, Martynas
  See also Mark

Marvin (Old English) sea friend
  Also Mervin, Mervyn, Merwin,
  Merwyn

Matong (Aboriginal) great and
  strong

Matthew (Hebrew) gift of the Lord
  Also Mata, Mateo, Mateusz,
  Mathaeus, Mathew, Mathhaus,

Mathias, Mathieu, Matteo,
Mattheus, Matthias, Mattias,
Matyas, Mayhew

Maurice (Latin) a Moor
Also Maolmuire, Mauricio,
Mauritius, Maurits, Maurizio,
Moritz, Morrell, Morris

Maximilian (Latin) the greatest
Also Maksimilian, Massimiliano,
Maxim, Maximilanus, Maximiliano,
Maximilien, Maximo

Maxwell (Old English) a large well

Maynard (Old German) strength and
hardy

Melbourne (Old English) from the
mill stream

Melvin (Irish) smooth brow
Also Malvin, Melvyn

Mervin *see* Marvin

Michael (Hebrew) one who is like
God
Also Micah, Michan, Micheil,
Michel, Michele, Miguel, Mihael,
Mihaly, Mikael, Mikhail, Mirko,
Mischa, Mitchell

Milan (Latin) the lovable

Miles (Old German) merciful
Also Milo, Myles

Milton (Old English) from the mill
town

Ming (Chinese) bright, brilliant

Mitchell *see* Michael

Montague (Old French) from the
pointed hill

Montgomery (Old French) from the
wealthy one's hill
Also Monty

Moonga (Aboriginal) dark

Morgan (Celtic) from the sea
Also Morgan

Morris (English) *see* Maurice

Moses (Egyptian) child
Also Moesen, Moise, Moises,
Moshe, Moyse, Mozes

Mullaya (Aboriginal) companion,
friend

Murdoch (Gaelic) sea man

Murray (Celtic) man of the sea

Myles *see* Miles

Myron (Greek) fragrant ointment

N

Nahum (Hebrew) comforter

Napoleon (Italian) of Naples

Narbethong (Aboriginal) cheerful, lively

Natan (Aboriginal) fig tree

Nathan (Hebrew) gift

Nathaniel (Hebrew) gift of God
Also Natanael. Nataniel, Nathanael

Ned *see* Edward

Neil (Irish) champion
Also Neal, Neale, Neall, Neel, Neill, Nels, Nial, Niall, Niel, Niels, Nigel, Niles, Nils

Nelson (English) son of the champion
Also Nealson, Nilson

Neville (French) new town
Also Nevil, Nevile

Nicholas (Greek) the people's victory
Also Claus, Miklos, Neacail, Niccolo, Nickel, Nickolaus, Nicodemus, Nicol, Nicolaas, Nicolas, Nicolo, Nikolai, Nikolay

Nicodemus (Greek) *see* Nicholas

Nigel *see* Neil

Nils (Scandinavian) *see* Neil

Ninian (Scottish) the name of a saint
See also Vivian

Noah (Hebrew) rest or comfort
Also Noach, Noak

Noel (Old French) Christmas
Also Natal, Natale, Newell, Nowell

Nolan (Irish) noble
Also Noland

Norman (Old English) northern man

O

Obadiah (Hebrew) servant of Jehovah

Oberon *see* Aubrey

Octavius (Latin) the eighth child
  Also Octavio, Ottavio

Olaf (Old Norse) ancestral relic
  Also Aulay, Olaff, Olav

Oliver (Old French) the olive tree, symbol of peace
  Also Oliverio, Olivero, Olivier

Omar (Arabic) highest, or first son

Orlando (Italian) *see* Roland

Orville (Old French) from a golden place

Oscar (Old English) God's spear
  Also Osgar, Oskar

Osmond (Old English) God's protection

Oswald (Old English) God's power

Othello (Italian) *see* Otto

Otis (Greek) keen of hearing
  Also Otys

Otto (Old German) rich
  Also Oddo, Odo, Othello, Otho

Owen (Welsh) well-born
  Also Owain, Owayne, Ywain
  See also Evan

P

Pablo (Spanish) *see* Paul

Paget (French) young attendant
  Also Padget, Page, Pagett, Paige

Pangalia (Aboriginal) eldest son

Paolo (Italian) *see* Paul

Pascoe (Middle English) born at
  Easter
  Also Pascal, Pascall, Paschal,
  Pasquale

Patrick (Latin) nobleman
  Also Padraic, Padraig, Padric,
  Padrick, Padruig, Patric, Patrice,
  Patricio, Patrizius, Patten

Paul (Latin) small
  Also Paavali, Paavo, Pablo, Paolo,
  Paulin, Paulo, Paulot, Pavel, Pavlos,
  Poul

Pedro (Spanish) *see* Peter

Percival (French) to cut through the
  valley
  Also Parsifal, Percy, Perseval,
  Persifal

Peregrine (Latin) wanderer
  Also Perry

Perry *see* Peregrine, Peter

Perseus (Greek) destroyer

Peter (Greek) stone or rock
  Also Farus, Feoris, Ferris, Peadair,
  Peadar, Peder, Pedro, Peer, Pekka,
  Per, Pero, Perren, Perrin, Perry,
  Pete, Petr, Petros, Petru, Petrus,
  Pierce, Piero, Pierre, Piers, Piet,
  Pieter, Pietro, Piotr, Pyotr

Phelan (Celtic) a wolf

Phelim (Irish) the ever good

Philip (Greek) lover of horses
  Also Felep, Felope, Filib, Filip,
  Filippo, Phelp, Philipp, Philippe,
  Phillip, Philp, Pileb

Phineas (Hebrew) oracle

Pierce *see* Peter

Piers (French) *see* Peter

Pikuwa (Aboriginal) saltwater crocodile

Piran (Irish) *see* Kieren

Pirramurar (Aboriginal) shield

Prentice (Old French) an apprentice
Also Prentiss

Preston (Old English) priest's place

Q

Quentin (Latin) the fifth child
   Also Quinn, Quinton

Quillon (Latin) sword hilt
   Also Quillian

Quincy (French) place name

Quong (Chinese) bright

R

Radcliffe (Old English) red cliff

Radford (Old English) red ford

Raleigh (Old English) red clearing
Also Rawley

Ralph (Old Norse) counsel and wolf
Also Rafe, Raff, Ral, Ralf, Raoul,
Rolf, Rolfe, Rolph

Ramsey (Old German) the strong
Also Ramsay

Randal *see* Randolph

Randolph (Old English) wolf's shield
Also Randal, Randall, Randell,
Randolf, Randolphus

Raoul (French) *see* Ralph

Raphael (Hebrew) healing by God
Also Rafael, Rafaelle, Rafaello

Raymond (Old German) wise and
mighty protector
Also Raimondo, Raimous, Raimund,
Raimundo, Ramon, Ray, Reamonn,
Redmond, Reymond

Raynor (Old German) mighty army
Also Rainer, Rainier, Rayner

Reece (Old Welsh) ardent one
Also Rees, Reese, Rhett, Rhys, Rice

Reginald (Old English) mighty,
powerful and forceful
Also Raghnall, Ranald, Regnaud,
Regnault, Reinald, Reinaldo,
Reinaldos, Reinhold, Reinold,
Reinwald, Renaldos, Renato,
Renault, Reynold, Reynolds,
Rinaldo, Roald, Ronald

Reuben (Hebrew) behold a son
Also Rube, Ruben

Rex (Latin) king

Reynard (Old German) mighty and
hardy
Also Raynard, Reinhard, Renard,
Renaud, Rennard

Rhys *see* Reece

Richard (Old German) hard ruler
Also Rhicert, Rhisiart, Ricard,

Ricardo, Riccardo, Richardus, Richart, Richerd, Riocart, Ryszard

Ringbalin (Aboriginal) song

Roald (Norwegian) *see* Reginald

Robert (Old German) bright shining fame
Also Bob, Hrodebert, Riobard, Roberto, Robertson, Robertus, Robin, Robinson, Rupert, Ruperto, Ruprecht

Robin *see* Robert

Rock (Old English) a rock

Roderick (Old German) famous ruler
Also Roderich, Roderigo, Roderikus, Rodrigo, Rodrigue, Ruaidhri, Ruik

Rodney (English) a place name

Roger (Old English) famous spear
Also Rodger, Rogerio, Rogero, Rogier, Rudigar, Ruggiero, Rutger

Roland (Old German) fame of the land
Also Orlando, Rodhlann, Roeland, Rolando, Roldan, Rollan, Rolland, Rollin, Rowland

Ronald (Scottish) *see* Reginald

Rory (Irish) red or ruddy

Roscoe (Old Norse) from the deer forest

Ross (Scotch Gaelic) from the peninsula

Rowan (Scandinavian) mountain ash tree

Roy (French) king
Also Rey, Roi, Ruy

Rudolph (Old German) famous wolf
Also Hrudolf, Rodolf, Rodolfo, Rodolph, Rodolphe, Rudolf, Rudolfe

Rudyard (Old English) from the red enclosure

Rufus (Latin) red-haired one

Rupert *see* Robert

Rupulle (Aboriginal) chief

Russell (Latin) red or rusty

Ryan (Irish) little king
Also Rhien

S

Sacheverell (Old French) kid gloves

Salvador (Spanish) the saviour
Also Salvadore, Salvator, Sauveur, Xavier

Samson (Hebrew) like the sun
Also Sampson, Sansom, Sanson, Sansone, Simpson

Samuel (Hebrew) heard by God
Also Samhairle, Sammel, Samuele

Sancho (Spanish) sanctified or holy
Also Santo

Sandy *see* Alexander

Saul (Hebrew) the asked or longed for

Scott (Old English) a Scotsman
Also Scotti

Seamus (Irish) *see* James

Sean (Irish) *see* John

Sebastian (Latin) the revered one
Also Bastian, Bastien, Sebastiano, Sebastien

Seth (Hebrew) substitute or compensation

Shane *see* John

Shannon (Irish) little old wise one

Sheridan (Irish) wild man

Sherlock (Old English) fair-haired, clear lake

Shiro (Japanese) fourth son

Shu-sai-chong (Chinese) happy all his life long

Sidney (Old English) from St Denis
Also Sydney

Siegfried (Old German) peaceful victory
Also Siffre, Sigfrid, Sigvard

Sigmund (Old German) protecting conqueror

Also Sigismond, Sigismund, Sigismundo, Sigismundus, Sygmunt

Silas (Latin) of the forest

Silvester (Latin) woody, from the forest
Also Sailbheastar, Silvestre, Silvestro, Sylvester

Simon (Greek) one who hears
Also Sim, Simeon, Simone, Siomonn

Sinclair (English) shining light

Solomon (Hebrew) peaceful
Also Salomo, Salomon, Solamh, Solamon Soloman, Solomone

Spencer (Old French) dispenser of provisions or storekeeper

Spiro (Greek) breath of the gods

Stanford (Old English) dweller by the stony ford

Stanislaus (Slavic) one who stands gloriously
Also Aineislis, Stanislas, Stanislav

Stanley (Old English) from the stony meadow
Also Stanleigh, Stanly

Stephen (Greek) crown or garland
Also Esteban, Estevan, Etienne, Istvan, Steaphan, Stefan, Stefano, Steffen, Stephanos, Stephanus, Stephenson, Steven, Stevenson

Stewart (Old English) steward or tender of the estate
Also Stuart

Sumner (English) one who summons by authority
Also Sumnor

Swain (Old German) a young man or boy in service

Sydney *see* Sidney

Sylvester *see* Silvester

T

Taber (Gaelic) a spring well

Tabor (Turkish) fortified encampment

Taffy (Welsh) *see* David

Talbot (Old English) a woodcutter
Also Talbott

Tancred (Old German) considered counsel

Tangari (Aboriginal) edible gum

Tate (Middle English) cheerful or joyful one
Also Tait

Teangi (Aboriginal) earthy

Ted/Teddy *see* Edward

Terence (Latin) smooth, polished one
Also Terencio, Terenz, Terry, Thierry

Thaddeus (Aramaic) praiser (Greek) stout-hearted, courageous

Also Taddeo, Tadeo, Tadhg, Thaddaus

Thane (Old English) courtier

Thanh (Vietnamese) tranquil, serene

Theobald (Old German) bold people

Theodore (Greek) God's gift
Also Feodor, Fyodor, Teodoro, Theodor, Theodous, Tudor

Thierry (French) *see* Terence

Thomas (Aramaic) a twin
Also Tamas, Tammany, Tammen, Tomas, Tomaso, Tomaz, Tomlin, Tuomas

Thor (Old Norse) strength
Also Thorold, Tor

Thornton (Old English) thorny town

Thurston (Danish) Thor's stone or jewel

Tiernan (Celtic) kingly

Timothy (Greek) honour and respect for God

Titus (Greek) safe; honoured
Also Tito

Tobias (Old English) God is good
Also Tioboid, Tobia, Tobiasz, Tobie, Toby

Todd (English) a thicket

Tonio *see* Anthony

Tony *see* Anthony

Tracy (Latin) bold, courageous one
Also Tracey

Travers (Old French) from the crossroads
Also Travis

Travis *see* Travers

Tremayne (Old Cornish) dweller at the stony town

Trent (English) place name

Trevor (English) great homestead

Tristan (Latin) the sorrowing
Also Drostan, Tristran

Tristram (Celtic) tumult or din

Troy (French) from the land of the people with curly hair

Trung (Vietnamese) faithful, loyal

Tuki (Aboriginal) bullfrog

Turuwun (Aboriginal) guard

Tuta (Aboriginal) parrot

Tynan (Irish) dark

Tyrone (Greek) sovereign, land owner

U

Ulric (Old English) wolf ruler
  Also Ulrich

Ulysses (Greek) hater of injustice

Uri *see* Uriah

Uriah (Hebrew) the Lord is my light
  Also Uri, Uria, Uriel

Uriel *see* Uriah

Uzziah (Hebrew) the Lord gives
  strength

V

Valentine (Latin) valiant and strong
one
Also Bailintin, Valentijn, Valentin,
Valentino

Valerian (Latin) strong and healthy
one
Also Valarius, Valerius, Valéry

Vance (Dutch) from
Also Van

Varian (Latin) capricious,
changeable
Also Varien, Varion, Varrian

Vassily *see* Basil

Vaughan (Celtic) little man
Also Vaughn

Vernon (Latin) to grow green and
flourish
Also Verne

Victor (Latin) victorious conquerer
Also Buadhach, Vitorio, Vittorio

Vincent (Latin) conquering
Also Vincente, Vincentio,
Vincentius, Vincenty, Vincenz,
Vinsionn

Virgil (Latin) flourishing
Also Virgilio, Virgio

Vito (Latin) alive, animated
Also Vitalis

Vivian (Latin) vital; alive
Also Vivien, Ninian

Vladimir (Old Slavic) glory of
princes

W

Wade (Old German) advancing

Wainbaru (Aboriginal) rain

Walden (Old German-English)
mighty ruler, usurper
Also Waldo

Wallabarl (Aboriginal) barking
lizard

Wallace (Scottish) a Welshman
Also Wallache, Wallis, Walsh,
Welch, Welsh

Walter (Old German) ruler of people
Also Galterius, Gauthier, Gautier,
Gualterio, Gualtiero, Ualtar,
Walther, Waltier

Wangarang (Aboriginal) tortoise

Ward (Old English) watchman,
guardian
Also Warde

Warner (Old German) protecting
warrior
Also Werner

Warreen (Aboriginal) wombat

Warren (Old German) watchman,
protecting friend

Warringa (Aboriginal) the sea

Warroo (Aboriginal) fire

Warwick (Old German) strong ruler
and defender
Also Warrick

Wayamba (Aboriginal) turtle
Also Wayembeh

Wayne (Old English) wagon-maker

Weeronga (Aboriginal) quiet one

Wen (Chinese) cultured

Wesley (Old English) of the west
meadow
Also Westleigh

Weylin (Celtic) son of the wolf

Wilbur (Old German) resolute and
brilliant

Willard (Old German) strong-willed or determined

William (Old German) resolute protector
Also Guglielmo, Guilhermo, Guillaume, Guillermo, Gwylim, Liam, Quilliam, Uilliam, Vilhelm, Viljo, Ville, Wiley, Wilhelm, Wilkes, Wilkie, Willem, Willis

Willis (Old English) *see* William

Wilmot (Old German) resolute spirit or heart

Winston (Old English) from a friend's estate

Wirake (Aboriginal) friend

Wirinun (Aboriginal) a sorcerer, clever person

Wirruna (Aboriginal) sunset

Withinka (Aboriginal) green frog

Wolfe (Old English) a wolf

Wolfgang (Old German) advancing wolf, progressive

Wollowra (Aboriginal) eagle

Woltsha (Aboriginal) eagle

Worippa (Aboriginal) storm bird

Wundurra (Aboriginal) warrior

Wylie (Old English) beguiling, charming

X Y Z

Xavier *see* Salvador

Xenos (Greek) stranger

Yael (Hebrew) strength of God

Yangoora (Aboriginal) stringy bark tree

Yarraan (Aboriginal) white gum

Yarran (Aboriginal) acacia

Yates (Old English) from the gates
Also Gates, Yeats

Yehudi (Hebrew) the praise of the Lord

Yemen (Japanese) guarding the gate

Yiannis *see* John

Yoland (Greek) the violet

Yularai (Aboriginal) satisfied

Yule (Old Norse) Christmas time
Also Yul

Yun (Chinese) fair and just

Yuri (Russian) *see* George

Yuroka (Aboriginal) sun

Yves (French) the archer
Also Ives, Ivo

Zachary (Hebrew) God remembered
Also Zacarias, Zacarius, Zaccaria, Zacchaeus, Zachariah, Zacharias, Zacharie, Zakarias, Zakarij, Zechariah

Zenas (Greek) God's gift

Zephaniah (Hebrew) God is darkness

Zev (Hebrew) deer
Also Zevie, Zvi